Vanity Fairs

Georg Franck

Vanity Fairs

Another View of the Economy of Attention

Springer

Georg Franck
Vienna University of Technology
Vienna, Austria

ISBN 978-3-030-41531-0 ISBN 978-3-030-41532-7 (eBook)
https://doi.org/10.1007/978-3-030-41532-7

This Springer imprint is published by the registered company Springer Nature Switzerland AG
The registered company address is: Gewerbestrasse 11, 6330 Cham, Switzerland

Preface

The emblem of vanity is the mirror. Allegorically, however, the emblem goes far beyond the image reflected in the mirrored glass. Vanity is the addiction of creatures who live their lives in the 'mirror' of the consciousness of their peers. What is reflected in this other consciousness is the attention being paid to us. The addiction concerns the obsession by knowing the precise amount of attention paid to us or to put it another way, the extent to which we feature in the consciousness of others.

The pursuit of attention is socially organized around what can be termed 'Vanity Fairs'. An introduction to the economy of attention with the title Vanity Fairs thus means addressing the economy as a kind of drug market. The competition for and exchange of attention, though all-pervasive in the lifeworld and by no means secret, has only recently been discovered by social theory. How could it have been hidden? It had to have found a conceptual hiding place in theory. In fact, there was a pretty good hiding place: the all-purpose concept of communication.

It is tempting to define communication reductively, as a mere exchange of information, thus omitting the fact that interpersonal communication always includes the exchange of attention. With that in mind, it was only logical that conceptualization of the economy of attention started with disentangling information and attention exchange in face-to-face communication. The context of its first articulation was an essay on the precision timing of turn-taking in conversation. The idea of the essay was not mine, but that of my sister Dorothea Franck, who was then engaged in the field of linguistic pragmatics. Her approach to conversation analysis was to replace the then common model of a grammar-regulated turn-taking with a model of implicit negotiation. Since I was working at that time on applying 'public choice' concepts to urban economics, she consulted me. The result was a model of conversation in which the exchange of information is underpinned by the exchange of attention. Turn-taking is negotiated implicitly by the participants, who invest their own attention as a scarce resource and take pains to be paid attention as a coveted income. With this dualism of properties, the concept of attention was connected to the heteronomous world of economic thought. Unexpectedly, the model proved to be viable. The economy of attention saw the light of day in a paper, co-authored by sister and brother, that appeared in *Papiere zur Linguistik* (Papers on Linguistics) in 1986.

When first tinkering with the idea of developing the concept further, I would never have imagined, nor did I even wish, that the economy of attention would have taken the trajectory it has. The idea, nevertheless, resonated too strongly with the change that was underway in the media world simply to be left on the shelf to gather dust. In developing its own dynamics in the back of the author's mind, it lured him away from his main responsibilities and compelled him to write two essays to be published in the German periodical *Merkur*. In 1989, an essay entitled 'The New Currency: Attention' and in 1993 another one headed 'The Economy of Attention' appeared. The die was cast when Carl Hanser Verlag, Munich, invited me to write a book on the topic.

In a sense, the book was premature. It was written in the main before the Internet appeared on the scene, though it was not published until 1998. In the meantime, the topic had independently made its way onto the World Wide Web. In 1997, Michel Goldhaber's 'The Economy of Attention and the Internet' appeared in the Internet journal *Next Monday*. It was from there that the concept started its career in the English-speaking world.

Meanwhile, a considerable body of the literature on the topic has sprung up, covering fields as diverse as economics and philology. What I cannot find, however, is an account of the addictive potential of attention—that is, of the all too human longing for playing a role in fellow humans' consciousness. I cannot believe that both this potential, and, respectively, desire, have been simply overlooked. What I see, rather, is a widespread reluctance to speak about consciousness in precisely the sense which must be considered in order to discuss the desire of playing a role in the consciousness of others. It is this kind of meaning, so goes the argument behind the common reservation, in which consciousness has no place in science. Indeed, any talk of a 'science of consciousness' rests on shaky grounds. Without dismissing these concerns, I nevertheless suggest turning the tables, asking whether the success story of the attention economy is not, in fact, waiting to be read as living proof of the very real power that is brought to bear by the desire to feature in others' consciousness.

Vienna, Austria Georg Franck
January 2020

Acknowledgements

The project of this book was preceded by a trial balloon: a paper with the title 'Vanity Fairs: Competition in the Service of Self-Esteem'. It appeared in the journal *Mind and Matter*, whose editor, Harald Atmanspacher, had invited me to submit it. Harald had already edited the first book on the economy of attention (long before *Mind and Matter* had seen the light of day) and has been of invaluable help in the author's excursions into what might one day become a science of consciousness. The project was finally sparked by a comment Katherine Peil Kauffman made on the paper and her encouragement to go deeper into the spiritual dimension of the economy of attention. Katherine, Psychologist, focused on the biology of emotion, brought in the key phrase of *natural spirituality*, which basically denotes sentience, this perfectly natural form of consciousness, but emphasizes its specific human formation.

The book would not have been completed without more than just a little help from friends. It was again my sister Dorothea Franck who decisively contributed to putting the project on the right track. She first donated the concept of emotional climate change and then was the first to work through the initial version of the manuscript. She detected a serious flaw and lent a generous helping hand in ironing out any dissonance of tone. In a later rescue operation, Sarah Spiekermann and Johannes Hoff saved me from a dead end I had run into. Sarah, Information Economist, corrected an over-optimistic picture of the citation process in science as a measurement process of pragmatic information. Johannes, Philosopher with a theological depth, convinced me of a reorganization of the structure of the treatise aimed specifically at the transition from the spiritual dimension of the capacity of conscious experience to the ethical dimension of the economy of attention. Sarah and Johannes earn a good portion of the architect's and therapist's fee for the remodelling of the structure. Robert van Krieken, Leading Sociologist of celebrity society, proved to be a very good critic by mixing a cocktail of wholehearted encouragement and subtle reservations regarding terminology. By making me aware of the risk I incur by replacing the term 'narcissism' with the more colloquial 'vanity', he inspired a reworking of the introduction that would have been omitted without his intervention.

There are three friends of mine who invested considerable time and effort to free me from the embarrassment in which a non-native speaker is in when writing not only papers in scientific pidgin, but a whole book in English: Silvia Plaza, Dwight Holbrook and Ross Ludlam. Silvia, having been my instructor for years, regrettably retired while the edit was still pending. She nevertheless took it upon herself to go through and extensively critique the still somewhat rudimentary draft of the introductory parts of the manuscript. Dwight, a fellow campaigner at the philosophical frontlines of the exploration of the ontology of presence, was exceptionally kind to take the time out of his life for face-to-face discussions regarding the entirety of a still-unfinished version of the manuscript on a full nine-day stay in Vienna. Ross, not only a native speaker but also a promising young author, did a terrific job of painstakingly editing the manuscript, attending to linguistic and argumentative consistency alike. He deserves recognition if the embodiments of a continental theorist have been turned into a book in English.

Most of all, I owe the completion of this book to the attentive awareness of my wife, Ingrid Schünemann. She understood me through my moments of vacillation and self-doubt more often than I did myself.

Contents

Introduction

What is more pleasant than the affectionate notice other people take of us, what is more agreeable than their compassionate empathy? What is more inspiring than addressing ears flushed with excitement, what is more captivating than exercising our own power of fascination? What is more thrilling than an entire auditorium of expectant eyes, what more overwhelming than applause surging up to meet us? What, ultimately, equals the enchantment sparked off by the delighted attention we receive from those by whom we are ourselves enchanted? The attention of others is the most irresistible of drugs. To receive it outshines receiving any other kind of income. This is why glory surpasses power, and why wealth is overshadowed by prominence.

This is also why it is becoming popular in our affluent society to rank income in attention above mere financial gain. When more and more people can afford the insignia of material wealth, then the desire for distinction will create a demand for attributes more selective than a high money income. In accordance with the law of the socialization of former luxury goods, such attributes will be found among the privileges of a still-recognizable elite. The undisputed common denominator of contemporary elites is celebrity. And celebrity is precisely the status of being a major earner of attention. When material wealth has become inflationary, then, according to the laws governing the expansion of human desires and aspiration, a re-orientation of social ambition is imminent (cf. Franck 1993/2018, p. 8).

Attention is an immaterial kind of income. Receiving attention means to play a role in the consciousness of another person. By being concerned about the role we feel to be playing in other consciousness we testify inadvertently that we deal with one another as embodied psyches, or to go one step further, as embodied souls. As embodied souls, we are doomed to wither in isolation. In order to blossom individually, we have to succeed in occupying both space and affection in fellow consciousness. What we thus testify, knowingly or not, is that the pursuit of attention has a spiritual dimension.

In theories about affluent society, even in those focusing on the growing popularity of attention income, the implications of the conscious nature of attention are hardly addressed. Instead of the spiritual dimension of the pursuit, the pathological

G. Franck, *Vanity Fairs*,
https://doi.org/10.1007/978-3-030-41532-7_1

dimension of the addiction is amply exposed. An early account of the growing dominance of the income in attention was significantly titled 'The Culture of Narcissism' (Lasch 1979). Narcissism denotes the self-centred ego's dependency on outer recognition. This dependency, by seeming to contradict the ego's preoccupation with itself, invites the suspicion of pathology. In psychology and in particular psychoanalysis, narcissism is described as a disorder, thus accounting for the indeed hard to tame antagonism of the ego's autonomy and dependency. The connotation of this antagonism with a disorder, however, must be carefully avoided when the addiction is selected as vantage point for a novel approach to the economy of attention.

An economy accounting for the spiritual dimension of attention is novel indeed, but it is interesting only if adding to our understanding of social reality. Spirituality adding to realism may look like a contradiction in terms. Arguably, however, accounting for people's concern about featuring in other consciousness is not. Colloquially, this concern is called vanity. Vanity, though deemed a vice, is a predisposition we all share. It is, though lacking a terminological definition, the common name for our congenital concern about our place in fellow consciousness. The reason why and the circumstances under which it deserves to be called a vice will be discussed in due course below. A reliable indication, however, that this concern is not without social relevance is the common place that the competition for attention occupies in everyday knowledge. Since it is close to a truism that there is little we care so much about as the role we feel to be playing in other consciousness, and since it is also plainly evident that the stage we long to play on is of limited space, we naturally assume that life in society involves an ongoing competition for attention. We thus intuitively understand what the trope of the vanity fair illustrates. The trope gives succinct expression to the market form that the competition for attention engenders. It is thus predisposed for visualizing how the individual's concern to feature in fellow consciousness organizes itself into a fully-fledged social economy.

If it looks frivolous to invoke an image as vulgar as that of the vanity fair for delineating an approach to the spiritual dimension of human coexistence, then that is quite in the spirit of the matter. The spiritual nature of consciousness is nothing elevated, let alone transcendent. We all live in the state of conscious presence—as long as we have not fallen into dreamless sleep or coma. We are all, by virtue of our sentient nature, intimately acquainted with what the term spirituality denotes. This knowledge by acquaintance even epitomizes what is so particular about our sentient nature. States of conscious presence are accessible only from within: from the perspective of the first person, i.e. in the perspective of the person who is themself mentally present. From the perspective of the third person, i.e. of the outside observer, they appear non-existent. No sentient being has ever inspected another's sphere of conscious experience. States of consciousness are be-ables[1], in contrast to observables (such as firing patterns of neurons or blood oxygen level dependency) by virtue of which the brain processes supposed to bring them forth are accessible to empirical methods. As be-ables, the states actually do exist, i.e. exist in the mode

[1] I take the wording from Pylkkänen (2014) who, in turn, refers to John Bell.

of presence, but they can be denied (physical) reality. This peculiar but nevertheless factual mode of existence is what the term spiritual basically refers to.

The air of mysteriousness surrounding the term is due to the fact that so far nobody knows how nervous systems manage to not only process information (i.e. to work as biological computers), but also to bring forth states of mental presence. Consequently, nobody has understood how and why our sensations, feelings and moods are made to present themselves as qualia, i.e. as phenomena that do not exist as observable objects, but only by being subjectively experienced. Science and thus neuroscience, by being committed to the perspective of the third person, are therefore rather stymied when faced by questions of conscious experience. Hence the inclination to explain the unexplainable away. Remarkably, however, this inclination is forcefully opposed from within science by a recent movement known as Toward a Science of Consciousness (TSC). One of the founding fathers of TSC, anaesthetist Stuart Hameroff, counters the scepticism succinctly: 'I know that consciousness exists since it is my job to take it away' (personal communication).

Vanity fairs still wait to be described as living proof of the existence of natural spirituality. Isn't it perfectly possible to interpret the sociologically manifest competition for attention as an informal, out-of-lab and large-scale experiment concerning the existential proof of that which eludes instrumental observation? Even in hardcore science, there are phenomena finding acknowledgement despite evading instrumental observation. The paradigm case is dark matter. Dark matter eludes observation as does sentience; it nevertheless is standardly acknowledged in cosmology for the reason of rendering the observation intelligible that the outsides of galaxies rotate too rapidly for either Newtonian gravity or general relativity to explain. Sentience, though certainly not acting as a substance, plays an analogous role in the endeavour of making sense of the well-observed economy of attention. It is hopeless to theorize this economy without referring to the motivational power of the anxiety about featuring in other consciousness. It is hopeless, in turn, to theorize this anxiety without accounting for the spiritual nature of both our own and other consciousnesses. Phenomenal consciousness, to make the somewhat daring comparison, is to attention economy what dark matter is to cosmology. Nobody has ever observed sentience as experienced subjectively, but it is good practice to deal with the capability, known by acquaintance, as a working hypothesis.

In a sense, of course, the comparison of consciousness with dark matter is just a continuation of that daring coupling of spirituality and vanity fairs. Take it as a tongue-in-cheek answer to the queer [scientistically bigoted] endeavour of explaining the spiritual away. It will not be made use of in the implementation of the argument: instead we will be satisfied with inserting the spiritual into the economic.

Retrospect: How Economic Theory Made Contact with the Heteronomous Subject of Attention

Economy, in its original and still basic meaning, concerns the selection of scarce means for given ends. Scarceness is to be distinguished from lack: it is a function of the multitude of possible uses of a means restricted in availability. Money is scarce because it can buy anything, but is controlled in total supply. Attention is scarce because it is needed for whatever one wishes to experience consciously while its capacity is constricted organically. Each dollar and each minute of mental presence, accordingly, can be spent only once. Each use for one thing costs the renunciation of all the other uses that would have been otherwise possible. Dealing not only with money, but also with one's capacity of conscious experience thus involves a problem of selectivity, highlighted in William James's classical definition of attention: 'Attention is the taking possession by the mind, in clear and vivid form, of one out of what seem several simultaneously possible objects or trains of thought. Focalization, concentration, of consciousness are of its essence. It implies withdrawal from some things in order to deal effectively with others, and is a condition which has a real opposite in the confused, dazed, scatterbrained state which in French is called *distraction*, and *Zerstreutheit* in German' (James (1890), vol. 1, pp. 403f).

James's definition immediately connects the capacity of conscious experience with economy. It was only logical, thus, that economic theory first took notice of attention in its property as a scarce resource. Herbert Simon opened his early account of what would later be called information society with the thesis that a society that is information rich is attention poor.[2] Simon, an economist and pioneer of artificial intelligence, is best known for introducing the concept of 'bounded rationality'. Bounded rationality accounts for the fact that decision making, contrary to the standard assumption of unbounded, i.e. 'homo oeconomicus'-type rationality, is not free of cost, but a resource-consuming activity. This relates most clearly to the process of dealing with information, since information is not fixed and ready-made, but the surprise value extracted from patterns by bestowing attention on them. That is why a wealth of information creates a poverty of attention. Attention, to put it differently, promises to play a key role in an economy focused on information. Even if defining information society in terms of the technology it idiosyncratically makes use of, it is precisely the technology that widens the bottleneck of attention's capacity of processing information.

Simon's account, nevertheless, was not responsible for bringing the term 'economy of attention' into the popular consciousness. His emphasis on the poverty of attention is biased insofar as the scarce resource is not the only property through which attention comes into contact with the economic. There is that other property, the quality we started from: generally coveted income. Attention is scarce when conceived as the capacity—or energy—that one disposes of; it turns into a source

[2] '[T]he wealth of information means a dearth of something else: a scarcity of whatever it is that information consumes. What information consumes is rather obvious: it consumes the attention of its recipients. Hence a wealth of information creates a poverty of attention' (Simon 1971, p. 40).

of delight when taken as a payment one receives from others. It was the observation that there is a kind of rivalry between money and attention income that gave rise to the now common conception of the economy of attention (Franck 1989, 1993/2018; Goldhaber 1997, Franck 1998). The observation was that of the rising significance of forms of wealth such as reputation, renown, prestige, prominence, and fame, that, without displacing material wealth entirely, dispute its monopoly as a measure of economic success.

The rivalry between money and attention income became most evident in the media world, where the economy of attention found its way into the business models of all the most successful corporations. Even before the internet, media such as commercial TV had left behind the selling of information (i.e. content), preferring to focus on the attraction of attention as a service to be sold to the advertising industry.

It was this change in the business world that eventually paved the way for the attention economy to become part of the core disciplines of economic thought, that is into mathematical economics (Falkinger 2005) and business administration (Davenport and Beck 2001). The tricky problem these approaches face lies in an appropriate definition of attention as a form of income. In contrast to money, attention is not a homogeneous means of payment. Its value is thoroughly individual: it depends first on the feelings it transports, and second on the esteem the receiver has for the payer. But individuality is not even the core problem. It is secondary compared to the subjectivity of both the payer and the payee. The feelings transported and the esteem involved are phenomena which do not come forth but in *conscious experience*, i.e. in states of mental presence. States of 'being there' consciously are accessible only from within: from the perspective of the first person. From the perspective of the third person, i.e. of the detached observer, they seem not to exist at all. No conscious subject has ever inspected a sphere of conscious experience other than its own. Science, however, and thus economics, is committed to the perspective of the third person. In order to be acknowledged as real, an entity's existence must be capable of being shown publicly (i.e. by empirical method or logical proof). Variables, accordingly, should be defined operationally, by way of describing the method by which they are measured or engendered. Phenomena that exist only by being experienced consciously—such as sensations, feelings, moods, sensory qualities; in short, qualia—are without a residence permit in the world of science. They belong to the sphere of experience that once was called the *soul*. Taken as the capacity of conscious experience, attention could hardly have been allowed to play the role as a resource, let alone a form of income, in economic theory. It was by a cunning of reason—or let us call it business acumen—that it obtained the permission nevertheless. The business model of new, i.e. advertisement-financed media, could leave the selling of information for money behind under the sole condition that the performance of the service of attraction was susceptible to measurement. Key to replacing the supply of information (as demanded by consumers) with services of attraction (as demanded by the ads industry) was the measurement of the performance of attraction in units such as audience ratings, circulation figures, page views and dwell times on websites. These kinds of measurement, far from being precise and doing justice to the individuality of the attention paid, nevertheless provide what business practice demands of an operational definition. They thus enabled economics and business administration to theorize, in their own terminology, the role that attention plays as income.

The price of the operational definition of attention income is that qualia, i.e. all those aspects of conscious experience that appear in the first-person perspective only, are abstracted away. The attention media count as income differs only nominally from time spent for media consumption. The definition is blank with regard to the emotional, let alone spiritual, dimension of attention; to the charm of feeling attended to, to the exhilarating potential of the drug. Packed into the tradable service of attraction, the good labelled attention elaborates nothing of the cult around attractiveness or about the market form it gives birth to. Attention *economics*, accordingly, has no concept of the vanity fair as epitomized by the literary trope to which the colloquial name owes its succinctness. The literary trope suggests a kind of fair or market, a socially organized competition for attention where a spectacle is supplied to catch eye or ear. In contrast to regular theatre, however, the ensemble of actors and the audience tend to be one and the same. Think of the proverbial theatre audience that wants to see and to be seen. The vanity fair is what takes place in the lobbies and foyers where the carefully styled appearance of visitors meets the critical review and the hopefully impressed attention of the others. There is quite a lot of effort and not least considerable expenditure invested in the outward display of the person and their appearance in the right surrounding. In literature, characteristically, the stakes tend to be even higher and the expenditures eventually ruinous. Because of the addiction to attention, the fair readily assumes the traits of a gambling den. The trope, in short, is supposed to illustrate both the source of energy that the pursuit of attention feeds on, and the corrupting force inherent in that most irresistible of drugs.

The trope, though far from a well-defined concept, swiftly collects the motives one has to start from when going into the collective results of the individual pursuit of attention. At the centre, of course, lies the motive called vanity. Vanity, to be sure, is no well-defined concept either. It is indispensable, though, for any deeper understanding of why wealth of attention plays, as it does, such a pervasive role in social life. Vanity is the unsurpassed expression for connecting the seemingly contradictory drives behind the pursuit of attention: the egotistic and the social impulse. Vanity, whether one takes it to mean excessive self-regard or just the craving for attention, denotes a drive that is both strongly self-centred and eminently social. It is self-centred since it is, in the last analysis, pursuit of self-esteem; it is eminently social since the self-esteem we can afford depends on our income of appreciative attention. At root of this dependency, to underline the point, lies the wishful imagination of playing a role in the consciousness of fellow humans.

General Economy Rather than Orthodox Economics?

By thus widening the horizon, the economy of attention loses its foothold in scholarly economics. This may seem not all too bad since there is an alternative format of economic theory: general economy. General economy, as theorized by Mauss (1925) and

Bataille (1967), generalizes the explicitly calculation-and-reward-oriented concept of economics by inquiring into the economic rationality of phenomena such as gift and squander. Vanity fairs, as commonly understood, are associated with frivolous luxuries and expensive display. They seem to belong to an economy of debilitating consumption rather than to the economy of value creation. Instead of investment as its aim, expenditure appears to end up in total loss once the bacchanal is over. An analogy to this concept of expenditure might be the common concept of a gift, where one does not expect a monetary reward or profit as a result of the handover. On the other hand, in a vanity fair a reward is expected from the expenditure, not unlike the American Indian ritual of the potlatch where an even greater reward is expected as a result of the gift. Potlatch is the paradigmatic case of general economy.

General economy, by being definitely humanities-minded, thus seems to be predisposed to theorizing an economy that is much more intuitive and aware of inner life, rather than one which merely involves the pure exchange of equivalents. General economy subordinates efficiency to squander, enrichment to sovereign generosity, prevailing in competition to overwhelming through gifts. Wealth of attention, according to general economy, is not waiting to be activated as capital, but is instead concerned with granting the chance of winning sovereignty and thus of developing elegance and noblesse. Vanity fairs, in potlatch mode, are displays of sovereign self-aggrandizement.

But doesn't sovereign self-aggrandizement mean that the pursuit of self-esteem has left behind all anxiety about esteem won from without? That self-esteem has emancipated itself from the dependency on other people's opinion? This emancipation, to be sure, is quite in the spirit of general economy. A general economic account of vanity fairs would much rather issue a flamboyant essay on the world of extravagance and transgression than a treatise on competition in the service of self-esteem. Among the reasons, though, why vanity fairs are so entertaining and iridescent is that they organize themselves as competitions. They work as informally organized beauty contests. Think again of that proverbial theatre audience: on their part, there is considerable investment in dress, in the adornment of the body and the styling of hair. There is certainly joy in sovereign spending and the exclusive satisfaction of one's own exact tastes. But it would be misleading to consider these expenditures as mere squander. It is equally certain, rather, that the expenditure is invested for the sake of gaining the attention of those in the audience to whom the spender themself is paying attention. Instead of facing idle luxury, we come across a model case of competition in the well-understood service of self-esteem.

Talk of investment smacks of utilitarianism and provokes rejoinders by advocates of the general economy school. Sovereign spending and unconditional generosity are no alternatives, however, when the pursuit of self-esteem is at issue. Sovereignty means independence of social control. Unconditional generosity means spending without expecting any kind of reward. You can dream of it as utopia, you can even argue that the dependency of self-esteem on foreign acclaim is a misery that calls for redemption. But you have to be clear that this dependency is not subjugation to an external power: it is innate, rather, and imposed from inside. Amalgamation of general economy and attention economy is blocked by the lack of the prospect of emancipating self-esteem from the dependency on esteem from outside. There is no way of deconstructing this dependency. Replacing the ego, bound to earn its living, with an ego sovereign in potlatch-style self-aggrandizement, would destroy the very rationality of the pursuit of attention. That the ego's self-esteem is subject to social proof does not mean, of course, that autonomy has to be sacrificed altogether. It means, rather, that autonomy and dependency have to be brought into balance somehow. The arduous and seemingly never-ending task of finding this balance is to the individual agent in the economy of attention what utility maximization is to the homo oeconomicus in orthodox economics.

Dealing with the Conscious Nature of Attention

What we are thus left with is the problem of how to account for the worth the ego attributes to itself in economic terms. The tricky point here is that self-esteem, in both its own nature and in what it depends upon, represents a phenomenon characterized by a very special *mode of existing*. It is a consciousness phenomenon, which means that it is something (if it can be called a 'thing') that exists only by virtue of being *present* in actual experience. Phenomena of consciousness do not come forth except in so-called *phenomenal states*, i.e. in states of mental presence. Mental presence is 'how it is' to be conscious. Phenomenal states are accessible only from within the consciousness they are phenomena of. Self-esteem is the epitome of what is called the *phenomenality*, to be distinguished from the *intentionality*, of consciousness. Intentionality of consciousness means that consciousness is always conscious *of* something. The meaning of intentional consciousness is covered by James's definition of attention, namely the consciousness that is capable of concentration and focalization. The phenomenality of consciousness, in contrast, refers to the very *feeling of being there*, to the feeling that mental presence has of its very being. Phenomenal consciousness is wherever, according to Thomas Nagel's famous definition, a feeling is present of 'what it is like to be' the being one is (see Nagel 1974). It thus may very well be that phenomenal consciousness can occur in much more primitive forms of life, unlike intentional consciousness, which, after all, presupposes objectifying perception or representational imagination. Phenomenal consciousness may be as primitive as the 'creature consciousness' that Chalmers (2000) defines as the most primitive form of conscious experience conceivable. Creature consciousness amounts to nothing more than the coming forth of a sensation without any differentiation as to a self that is sensing and a content that is sensed. In creature consciousness, the sensation of what is present and the self-sensation of presence are one. The presence of a sensation, however primitive and dim it may ever be, amounts to a feeling of *one's own being there:* a feeling of one's own as it is implied in the very meaning of 'being conscious'.

Self-esteem is a somewhat elaborated feeling of being the creature one is, heavily crossed by intentionality. It is not just feeling good or bad; nor does the 'how it feels' exclusively depend on outside esteem. Answering the question 'what do I look like to myself?' rather asks for judgment and deliberation. This enrichment of phenomenal consciousness by intentionality does not, however, overshadow the basically phenomenal nature of the sense of self—it just connects to the capabilities covered by the concept of mind: imagination, cognition, thought, planning, intelligence. It is thus interesting to see what drops out of the concept of mind when theorized, as done by the science-minded philosophy of mind, in purely intentional terms. By abstracting the 'how it feels' qualities away, the mind finds itself reduced to the capability of selectively processing information, a capability encountered wherever computation takes place. This reduction was hailed in science-minded philosophy and psychology alike, insinuating that the human mind could be considered to be a biological precursor of artificial intelligence. For our purpose the reduction is informative, in that it draws a sharp line between intentionality and phenomenality. AI, however closely it may simulate human behaviour, will never incorporate what is most succinctly expressed by the old-fashioned notion of the soul.

The soul is what feels good or bad depending on the feelings it presumes to encounter in other souls of its own species. The 'how it feels' quality is key to understanding the nature of self-esteem and the charm of being paid attention alike. With only intentional consciousness there can be no magic of feeling adulation or praise from others. What makes us thoroughly addicted to attention is that its reception includes the promise of being welcomed in a soul that seems to *be* an experiencing subject as we ourselves are—and the attention it pays is charged with emotions as is our own.

By clinging to the reductive concept of mind, even Harold Pashler's still standard Psychology of Attention (1998) turns a blind eye to what attention means as psychic income. In Pashler's definition, attention is reduced, without reservation, to the capacity of selectively processing information, thus made susceptible to measurement in terms of information theory (computer science). Any ideas of accounting for the relationship between the pursuit of attention and self-esteem are thus scotched from the very beginning. The ideal endgame of the pursuit of attention is certainly not having one's personal data processed by the neural machinery of non-sentient zombies, but being welcomed in a soul of the very same nature as one's own. It would be a major offence to self-conscious vanity if it were fooled by a robot that only mimics conscious behaviour.

Pashler's psychology and the orthodox economists' approach to attention are in accordance regarding the operational definition and thus the conceptualization of attention as a variable suited to enter mathematical modelling. By this pruning, though, just those qualities are abstracted away that the pursuit of attention primarily concerns. Attention, defined as that which is measured, be it in terms of audience statistics or information theory, has only faintly to do with that from which self-esteem lives. Both psychology and economics of attention have thus taken themselves out of the project of theorizing the economy of attention in the proverbial meaning that the concept has assumed by now.

There is no embarking on such a project without escaping the Procrustean bed of operationalism. Yet, no economic approach whatsoever can simply disregard measurement. There is no economic account of attention as a form of income that could do without accounting for how the precious good is subject to some kind of gauging. An economy of comprehensively understood attention, therefore, has a measurement problem of its own. The problem lies in gauging the weight and extent of the role one plays in the consciousness upon which one is anxious to make an impression.

Gauging the space one occupies in other consciousness is key to any economic account of the pursuit of attention. In such a type of economy, information about the relevance of the role one plays in other consciousness takes the place the operational definition occupies in reductive theories of attention. It is key to accounting for dependent self-esteem in economic terms. Since it must cope with the inaccessibility of consciousness from outside, the format of its measurement problem is quite formidable. It is easy, even, to argue that there is no way to a solution. Other, or foreign (phenomenal type) consciousness, to begin with, can neither logically nor empirically be proved to exist at all. Even though we have good reason to assume that other people embody a consciousness of our own kind, it is theoretically possible, so goes the argument, that our fellow humans are zombies, i.e. organisms that are behaviourally identical to humans but lacking conscious experience.[3] The theory that consciousness is nothing but a subjective illusion is quite popular in quarters of neuro- and techno-science. There are serious philosophers claiming to see no difference between themselves and biological robots—'We are robots born of robots born of robots ...' philosopher Daniel Dennett proclaims (see Dennett 1994). For those who profess to be robots, viewing humans as embodied souls is a metaphysical superstition based on the unresolved remains of religious faith.

For people feeling unable to doubt that they are de facto mentally present and consciously aware, the doubt that their fellow humans embody a soul amounts to confessing to solipsism—a confession which, if taken seriously, is even harder to perform than the exercise of forswearing the drug of attention. Those self-professed robots, accordingly, prefer to doubt that they themselves are acquainted with phenomenal states. What they overlook is that this doubt is nothing less than self-defeating. You can get rid of phenomenal consciousness by undergoing anaesthesia or falling into dreamless sleep, but you cannot declare mental presence an illusion without being actually in the state of mental presence. You can insist, of course, on a definition of reality that includes as a necessary condition of the acknowledgement of something as real that it is accessible in the perspective of the third person. But you may be too quick in presupposing that there are no external indications whatsoever of the facticity of mental presence. Those denying the existence of the phenomenal do not themselves differ from humans aware of their mental presence when it comes to earning attention. They do not even hesitate in dancing to the tune of vanity, but rather enjoy finding themselves regarded by those they themselves regard. They are frustrated when their lectures are poorly attended and their papers are poorly cited. They deny in words what they testify in deeds.

---

[3] *The Journal of Consciousness Studies*, vol. 2, no. 4, 1995, pp. 312–372 reports the symposium where the Zombie debate started. Authors are, among others, Owen Flannagan, Daniel C. Dennett, Jaron Lanier, Avshalom C. Elitzur.

Warding off doubts about the very existence of phenomenal consciousness is only a preliminary step in tackling the gauge problem. The actual problem is not so much of a theoretical as of a practical nature. Those feeling dependent on attention income have to cope with the circumstance that the role they would like to play in another consciousness is always only staged in their own imagination. Living one's social life in the mirror of other people's consciousness means to take over the first-person perspective of others in one's own imagination.

So the question becomes that of how exactly we look into the mirror. To put it bluntly: the look is seeing by virtue of an act of faith. By believing that we share our exclusive first-person perspective with those around us we find ourselves able to switch perspectives imaginatively and empathetically. The act of faith is not something that has to be performed explicitly. Our instinctive longing for being loved—at least by those we love ourselves—suggests that the belief in the existence of the other soul is pre-reflective and pre-rational. Nobody wonders that even those revoking the belief explicitly are heartbroken if not allowed to believe tacitly to be playing a privileged role in at least one other consciousness.

Looking at the behaviour we observe from outside as if looked at from within means to project our necessarily own subjectivity behind the appearance vis-à-vis. This projection, as promising as it is daring, is an act of jumping the abyss. It is promising since it opens up the possibility not only of observing behaviour but understanding it. It is daring since almost inevitably one is also projecting one's prejudices, unconscious presets and idiosyncrasies. The act of faith nevertheless does wonders in putting our empathetic capabilities as well as our insatiable desire for sense and coherence to work in the service of understanding. Empathy, far from being just acquired, is deeply ingrained in our physical constitution. Humans and indeed a range of other creatures have mirror neurons in their brains. Mirror neurons induce the motor cortex to reproduce the motor programme corresponding to the posture or activity identified by the visual perception of another organism (see Rizzolatti and Craighero 2004 for the original discoverers' account). We feel, in other words, how our counterpart feels in their skin. We are naturally born empathizers; but empathy, like other intuitive gifts, is open to education, thus to elaboration and refinement, as well as to dulling and deformity. The best proven way of weakening one's prejudices and preconceptions in empathizing lies in making extensive use of the desire for sense and coherence. There is no better way of looking at other people's behaviour in their own perspective than insistently and tenaciously searching for that one interpretation that makes the most coherent and consistent sense in the given context and situation. There is no better way of overcoming one's prejudices than this 'charitable interpretation'.[4]

How does this relate to the gauge problem concretely? It means, first of all, to realize that the main source of bias and imprecision in assessing the role one plays in another consciousness is wishful thinking. Since it is always only in our own imagination that we access the first-person perspectives of those around us and since,

[4]Davidson (1974). To be treated more extensively in Chapter "Moral Elegance: An Ethics Tailored to Vanity Fairs?".

in addition, addiction is in play, it is all too easy to fall victim to wishful thinking. Vanity as such can be described as a strategy of wishful embellishment of the role one would like to believe to be playing in the consciousness one has in mind. The most convenient way of indulging in the seduction is to rely on verbal assurances of esteem. Realism in gauging one's role thus requires us, first of all, to neutralize wishful thinking. It means, to be specific, to ask whether there is a language for expressing preferences in which it does not pay to lie. Such a language indeed exists and we inevitably and inadvertently make use of it. It is a constitutive part of the economy of attention, relating, as it does, to the property of attention as a scarce resource. Words are cheap, attention is not. Each minute of attention we pay to one thing comes at the expense of other things we have to forego as alternative possibilities. Our expenses of attention, intended or not, reveal our preference order (which resonates in economics with Paul Samuelson's (1947) theorem of the revelation of preferences by preparedness to pay).

By dispensing with alternative possibilities, our expenses of attention show where our real concerns lie. The use of our attention discloses more than a thousand words can deny. The husband may assure his wife a thousand times that she is his one and only, but if he never brings her the flowers she loves so much and also forgets their anniversary, she might well wonder whether she is the sole object of his love. The way we use our attention betrays our real interests like a lie detector. A realist in the case of asseverated appraisal is she who unaffectedly counts on the revelation of the preference structure through evinced preparedness to pay.

The gauge problem thus reduces to reading outward behaviour as an expression of the allocation of attention behind it. This reading is much more about divining and deciphering than straightforward comprehension, requiring some detective sense. But it does not demand all too much from socially normal people. They have been in training since early childhood. Babies already react to the mother's slips of inattentiveness. We all have acquired a fine sense for being listened to by only half an ear. It goes without saying that assurance of love wants to be backed by a reading of wishes before they are uttered. Jealousy lets us know that each one of us has what it takes to be a master detective in reading the balance sheet of attention households. The know-how to draw conclusions from overt behaviour about internally allocated attention lies at the heart of social intelligence. The scope and precision of the insight taken depend on the effort, i.e. on the attention bestowed on the inquiry.

Detective reading of outward behaviour is a makeshift, certainly when considered as a way of gauging the space some thing or person occupies in the consciousness of others. Since direct inspection of the other mind is denied, it is only ever circumstantial evidence it can provide. This weakness, however, entails a potential the activation of which has given rise to nothing less than the most recent thrust of innovation in the media business. Circumstantial evidence, its makeshift nature notwithstanding, is susceptible to massive support through automated methods of data acquisition and data analysis.

When looking for kinds of behaviour that promise to be particularly illuminating with regard to the allocation of attention, and which, on the other hand, are also suitable for methods of social survey, the use of media is certainly a leading choice. Media use without devoted attention is pointless: the observation thereof, accordingly, was key to the development of advertisement-financed media. Though sufficient for the practical purposes of mass media such as commercial TV, the audience ratings that the social survey of media use started with are a rather coarse and summary method, blind as they are to the individual preference structures that the detective reading of interpersonal exchange is out to decipher. Things changed with the advent of interactive media, i.e. the internet. Portals providing access to an endlessly searchable internet could hardly be prevented from developing into observation stations suited to record the users' individual behaviour down to the minutest detail. Add services for posting, sharing and communicating content, and you find the survey extended to the social graph: to the net of exchange relations and thus to the social distribution of the attention fed into the net. Circumstantial evidence thus turns into a panoptic overview of the networked flows of the attention absorbed by the media.

The flows of attention soaked up and channelled through the media are only a section, of course, of the social economy of attention. This section, nevertheless, is a sample that becomes increasingly representative the more popular the so-called social media becomes. The more people get used to communicating and doing their daily business via Google, Facebook, Twitter and co., the more extensive the yield of data and the more powerful the techniques of pattern recognition by big data analytics become. Broken down to the level of the individual, the patterns coming to light are not just habits of media use, but preference structures as revealed by the payment of attention. The preference structures, as reflected in the user data, are statistical constructs that lack the colouring and dazzling vividness of the complex formations that personal interaction can reveal. Still, the scantness of the parametric model is counterbalanced by the extended possibilities of data analysis. Most importantly, however, the data, through being appropriated by the media operators, are thereby edited for automated mass screening.

We have arrived at—or, rather, passed—a turning point. The roaring success of social media provides the 'smoking gun' kind of evidence that it is very possible to gauge the space which some thing or person occupies in foreign consciousness. The figurative gun, however, has a treacherous double meaning. It does not just illustrate the weight of evidence provided by social media's resounding success—but also alludes to the danger inherent in the knowledge of our preferences (and indeed other, sundry details) thus becoming available. The turning point is marked by a shattering ambiguity. The knowledge falling into the lap of social media may be discerned as an empiricism that an economics or, respectively, econometrics of attention can only dream of. But as soon as it obtains to actual quality of life in the pertinent social reality, the dream swiftly becomes a nightmare as the metaphorical gun is turned on the user. A science emulating the screening, so far operated by privately owned media, would mean that the knowledge base, until now monopolized by privately owned corporations, is either published and thus made accessible to the general public or classified and thereby turned into a state secret. Either way would seal the end of privacy, this centrepiece of civil rights.

Privacy, of course, is under threat long before large-scale surveillance becomes a reality. Renunciation of the exclusive sanctity of one's private sphere is the entrance fee one has to pay to become a member of the user community. In the online world, one's home is no longer one's castle. The price is pretty high; there must be a particular reason why so many people are prepared to pay it. What does one get in turn for allowing oneself to be spied upon? Supply of online information as a consumer good is certainly too weak a stimulus for explaining the sweeping popularity of Facebook, Instagram and the like. You don't need these platforms for searching or surfing the net, for accessing online news or videos, for browsing lexicons and encyclopaedias online. There must be something satisfying stronger needs and wants than those that can be fed with information—longings sufficiently strong to explain the downright addiction evinced by users who constantly check their accounts for followers, friends and likes. The indeed exclusive offer of the social networks and the real 'kick' of their use lies in the opportunity they provide to earn attention. What you get is the opportunity to enter, in the most convenient way possible, the business of publishing information, including measurement and accounting of the attention it attracts. This is the offer so many people feel unable to refuse, serious privacy concerns notwithstanding.

With social networks, vanity fairs have gone online. They are the largest such fairs ever observed,[5] encompassing over one third of the world population. Though the exact price to be paid in terms of what is required to overcome privacy concerns among users might escape quantification, the figures of the total time absorbed by the media are a meaningful proxy measure of the attention turned over. The figures thus represent a first statistical measure of the relevance vanity fairs have in present-day society. The figures, of course, cover only a recently emerged submarket of the social economy of attention. These figures, though far from being representative regarding the relevance the pursuit of attention has in society at large, are good for providing a rough idea of the very quantum of psychic energy turned over on the drug market of attention.

Itinerary of the Exploration

The fact that phenomenal states are shielded against inspection from outside has never prevented people from competing for space in other people's consciousness. Indeed, occupying this space is what we are by our very nature addicted to. Occupying this space means getting the attention of its owner. What makes us a lifelong addict is the fact that self-esteem is deeply ingrained in our emotional self-regulation. The most natural starting point of a non-reductive account of the economy of attention is therefore the psychic household in the purview of which the revenues of attention

[5] 1.56 billion people on average log onto Facebook daily and are considered daily active users (Facebook DAU) for March 2019. This represents an eight per cent increase year on year (Source: Facebook as 4/24/19). For 2018, the figures reported are: users spend about 950 million hours on Facebook each day. With 2.13 billion monthly users and 1.4 billion daily users, that means the average monthly user spends 27 min per day in the app, and if you go by daily users, they spend about 41 min per day on Facebook. (Source: zephoria.com/top-15-valuable-facebook-statistics/06.02.2018).

are converted into the asset of self-worth. Chapter I "Competition in the Service of Self-esteem", goes into the accounting of this conversion, including the tricks of false accounting it provides opportunity for. Opportunism and strategic rating in this accounting are what separate fair play in the pursuit of attention from the foul play of vanity and resentment. The questions thus tackled are: To what exactly is the morally pejorative undertone in the meaning of vanity fair due? How are vice and virtue interrelated in the pursuit of self-esteem? What are the costs and risks of utilizing attention as an incentive to socially desirable behaviour? The discussion will entangle us in considerations of how the intra-psychic household of self-esteem connects to the social economy of attention, of how the social dependency of the ego relates to its self-assuredness, and of how self-esteem tackles the antagonism of autonomy and dependency.

The antagonism of autonomy and dependency reappears as a characteristic trait of the social fields where competitions for attention traditionally perform responsible work. The tension arises from the differences between culture and commerce. Commerce deals with things for reasons of economic gain, i.e. for ends different from those embodied in the things themselves. Culture, in contrast, is supposed to deal with things for their own sake. The paradigmatic case is art. Even though art can be dealt with as merchandise, artistic practice is supposed to be autonomous, i.e. serving only self-selected purposes and rules.

By emancipating itself from the supply of merchantable decoration and embellishment services, art could grow into the great laboratory for the research of latent desires of taste, i.e. of desires that cannot be recognized but by fulfilment. This emancipation would have been pointless, however, had it meant to escape any control whatsoever. The claim of autonomy corresponds to that of extraordinary inventiveness. Chapter II "The Emergence of Canons", goes into the question of how this claim can be verified. High claims make sense only if relying on selection processes that go further than just discriminating between insignificant material and valid work. Such high claims must be backed by an established ranking of works according to performance.

It would be easy to find arguments against the sheer possibility of such a ranking. A ranking that is binding amounts to nothing less than the social objectification of the judgement of taste. Taste, as everybody knows, is subjective. Incredibly, though, there is widespread consensus among experts about a selection of artworks that satisfy the highest standards of aesthetic quality. Each classical discipline of art owes its classic status to a catalogue of classics, the so-called canon.

The selection process behind the catalogues is a well-orchestrated, multi-level competition for attention that foregoes formal organization, however. It gives a first impression of what vanity fairs are capable of when put to responsible use. The frivolous mood of the vanity fair is noticeable in the selection of classics only insofar as the art business is so societal, iridescent and entertaining.

In art theory and art history, the selection process of paradigmatic quality is dealt with under the heading of discourse, which is appropriate insofar as the competition among experts can be described as an exchange of arguments about aesthetic judgement. The problem with this view is that experts never agree as long as they exchange arguments at all. It is only after having left debate behind that the so-called discourse gives birth to those uncontested classics. The discourse of art, as I will argue in Chapter II "The Emergence of Canons", is a misnomer. The discourse is not an exchange of information in the first place, but a market where information is exchanged for the attention of an art-appreciating audience. What counts is the number of exhibitions, of reviews in reputed media, treatises in the literature on art history, in textbooks, lexicons and university curricula. A given work is a classic not before it is unavoidably met in the authentic and binding compendia of the history of art.

The selection process of paradigmatic aesthetic quality is a highly remarkable market in the economy of attention. It is as old as is connoisseurship in artistic quality. Catalogues of classics, accordingly, date back to antiquity. The classics of Greek antiquity are classics of Roman antiquity, are classics of Renaissance, and are finally classics to this day, occasional cultural upheaval notwithstanding. The catalogue of classics, though in constant change regarding internal ranking, is close to being perfectly stable regarding the membership directory. This stability is remarkable as such; it is all the more amazing when one considers that the catalogue's management is only loosely institutionalized. There are museums dedicated to the public exhibition of classics, but there is no authority in charge of securing the selection process. The selection of classics can be taken as the archaic form of the vanity fair put to socially responsible use.

Care of tradition, nevertheless, did undergo some kind of institutional development. Art history took shape as a literary genre in the Renaissance. It became a scholarly discipline in the 19th century. Even though it is only loosely covered by citation indexing, there is informal monitoring of the citation process by overview gained in research.

With the institutional development of art history, we have tacitly changed the subject. We have landed in the field of academic research, another heavyweight in the cultural sector. Academic research, though sharing some borders with artistic research, is in contrast a formally organized and strongly regulated branch of knowledge production. There is, nevertheless, a consistent commonality: the use of a vanity-fair type of self-regulation. The core sector of self-imposed regulation is science, the subject of Chapter III "Scientific Communication: A Vanity Fair?" The output of scientific production is not (or at least only in exceptional cases) sold for money, but published and thus delivered free of charge. Scientists are supposed to work for epistemic gain, another motive to do things for their own sake. Science differs from art, however, in much more than the interest in knowledge. Since early modernity the scientific system of knowledge production has undergone a massive institutional, technological and moreover economic development, resulting in a transformation of collaborative research into an industry where specialized lines of production produce inputs for other specialized lines of production. An industry thus differentiated relies on the reintegration of the specialized lines through markets that couple exchange with evaluation of the output. It is only by this coupling of exchange and valuation that the advantages of the division of labour can be fully exploited. The conditions for the possibility of this coupling had first to be developed, however.

They were realized in the form of another vanity fair put to socially responsible use: the exchange of scientific information for expert attention that we today call scientific communication.

The development of scientific publication goes back to early modernity and coincided roughly with a revolutionary technological innovation in the economy of thought. Thought economy is that part of the economy of attention that deals with attention in the property of a scarce resource. The capacity of attention for dealing with mental objects is frighteningly narrow and plainly unable to deal with objects of the complexity of scientific theories if not equipped with a technology that greatly magnifies efficiency. In early modernity, Descartes's rational method was coded for dealing with problems that are much too complex for being grasped at once; observation was supplanted by measurement qua experimentation; mathematics was fully made use of as the language of theorizing.

Division of cognitive labour and technological progress in thought economy lie at the base of the sweeping success of modern science. Key to the division of cognitive labour and to a self-organizing tendency towards efficiency, however, is the market where information is exchanged for attention. It is due to the fundamental role of this market that science could grow into a closed economy of attention, where scientists invest their own attention for getting the attention of others, thus joining the use of attention in its property as a scarce resource to its use in the property of a means of gratification. Since a piece of information assumes scientific value only by being paid attention within the scientific community, scientists are supposed to work not only for epistemic gain, but also for the wage of fame.

Chapter IV "The Economy of Attention in the Age of Neoliberalism", turns to the recent adaptation of the market form of scientific communication by the media industry. Media such as books, press, cinema, TV and the internet are information markets that can be divided into old media and new media according to market form. Old media are those markets where information continues to be exchanged for money, new media are those having left the sale of information behind to focus solely on the attraction of attention. New media finance themselves by selling the service of attraction to the advertising industry. The market form of scientific communication thus finds itself translated from a highly differentiated producers' market into an information market for mass consumption. This adaptation proves stunningly successful. New media outperform old media wherever they meet in competition. The business model of supplying information for the payment of attention instead of money lies at the foundations of the highest-priced firms on the planet. Advertisement-financed media have turned the economy of attention into the most successful business model of the 21st century.

In the business of mass attraction, the best proven attractor is the display of wealth of attention, i.e. the presentation of celebrities. Celebrities are paid attention for the talents that once triggered their career, but also, if not in the first place, precisely for having accumulated so much wealth. Wealth of attention finds itself activated as an interest bearing capital. With the professionalization of mass attraction, the economy of attention thus assumes traits of capitalism. Since the fortunes to be displayed have first to be built up—and since the media are the only authority with the masses of attention necessary for elevating candidates to the peerage of prominence at their disposal—the media also enter the business of finance by granting credits in terms of attention. The economy of attention thus brings forth a mental kind of capitalism.

Mental capitalism developed in remarkable synchrony with the emergence of so-called financial industries in money-driven economy. Financial industries differ from traditional finance in that they leave the retail trade of loans behind, only to package shares in credits given into derivative capital, the acquisition of which entitles one to subscription for profits. New media, accordingly, no longer satisfy the demand for information, entertainment etc. in the first place, but package the attraction power of the information supplied into the derivative form of a saleable service. In both cases, we are dealing with a second-order kind of capitalism, hovering over rather than resting on the real base of the economy.

Mental capitalism, its tendency for self-rule notwithstanding, remains firmly tied to the source of its primary energy. Its real base is what the financial power of the advertising industry relies on. Advertising, though adding nothing to its tangible properties, is supposed to manipulate perception of the expected utility value of the product. The best proven means of captivating the expectations of prospective consumers lies in counselling how to make other people take note. This counselling is what advertising and, in particular, branding is mainly about. The huge complex of industries financed by the advertising industry thus serves, in the last analysis, the utilization of consumption for the pursuit of attention. Or, put the other way round, the real base of mental capitalism is the preparedness of consumers to buy the promise of attractiveness. It was by elaborate exploitation of consumers' endeavour to play the longed-for role in other consciousness that the cult around attractiveness could take the form of an attraction-industrial complex, which eventually took over both commerce and culture. This takeover resonates with the worst fears of late-modern cultural criticism. The absorption of culture by cultural industry was the nightmare of a conception of art that considers it inconceivable to tolerate non-artistic motives in autonomous art.

Chapter V "Deconstruction and the Fusion of Culture and Commerce", turns to the reaction of autonomous art to the fusion of culture and commerce characteristic of mental capitalism. The broadest and, at the same time, most pointed reaction of art discourse to the no longer sustainable banishment of non-artistic motives from autonomous art was a nouvelle vague of criticism heralded as deconstruction. Deconstruction, instead of exacerbating certain lines of cultural criticism, set out to shake the idea of certainty as such. The nouvelle vague, though flooding the postmodern discourse of art across disciplines, was translated into artistic practice most directly in architecture, where it became emblematic of postmodernism. Deconstruction in architecture denotes the theoretically relined design strategy of demonstratively subverting hitherto unshakeable certainties. Its striking success, Chapter V "Deconstruction and the Fusion of Culture and Commerce" argues, is due to the demonstration of how autonomous art can catch up with the media's professionalism of attraction without having to descend to the lowlands of mass attraction.

The policy of protecting fine-tuned attraction against slips into populism consisted of replacing the discrimination between artistic and non-artistic motives in art production with the discrimination between kinds of attention that artists have to compete for in pursuing an artistic career. By relying on this latter discrimination, art could afford to be excessively spectacular as long as it cared to selectively address an art-affiné, i.e. aesthetically and intellectually educated audience. Emblematic of this shift in the demarcation of art and cultural industry is the star architect, the incorporation of the architect into celebrity culture without depriving their profession of its distinctive artistic claim.

The fascination with stardom is hard to distinguish from fetishism, with figures and rankings supposed to measure the wealth of attention. Such fetishism, a hallmark of celebrity culture, has already begun its occupation of the art world. Yet, rather than installing itself as a role model of artistic creation, it has occupied art as a sector of cultural business. Celebrating the spell of figures and rankings is the privilege of commercial culture. Artistic exploration is expected to decipher the alienation that the fetishism amounts to.

Addressing the alienating effect of commercialization is not the same as invoking social criticism. True, commercialization includes a subordination of psychic households to external rule. The fascination with quantity, however, is not just imposed from outside. It is of endogenous origin as well. It goes back to the insatiability of the longing for attention. It has to do with the very nature of vanity. The intermediate form between mindful adequacy and alienating abstraction is the fascination with wealth. The longing for attention all too easily grows into the desire to get more than one can return. As soon as the longing reaches this quantitative goal, the nature of what the pursuit is aiming at inadvertently changes. Attention finds itself aligned with the principle 'the more the better'. There is a tipping point where empathetic awareness tilts into a streamlined preoccupation with enrichment.

Vanity, in its problematic meaning, refers to the germ of degeneration that the pursuit of attention carries within it. The pursuit is instinctive, but the degeneration goes back to self-inflicted immaturity. We face a complementarity like that of an original sin: a predisposition that is both inborn and ethically relevant. Complementarity means that there are properties which are, though ostensibly incompatible, both necessary for describing the phenomenon completely. Vanity's complementarity has consequences for a description of the attention economy under the heading of Vanity Fairs. The description would have to remain incomplete without reconsidering the ethical dimension of vanity. Yet, ethics and social theory are incompatible in turn. Even if not insisting on value-free theorizing, it is more than problematic to infer from the normative 'ought' to the 'is' of the matter of fact. A less problematic way of doing justice to this quandary might thus be to ponder the idea of an ethics tailored to a lifeworld that is under the sway of vanity fairs. Put more modestly, a way of accounting for the ethical dimension of the economy of attention might lie in addressing the question of whether the idea of such an ethics indeed makes sense.

Alienation and fetishism, of course, are not the only effects of commercialization that are of ethical concern. Nor do the mass media, having given rise to celebrity culture, any longer represent the high end of the commercialization of attention economy. New media have in their own turn undergone a split into older mass and recent interactive media. With social media, as the interactive media are called, the ecological dimension of the economy of attention becomes apparent. Ecological concerns inevitably involve ethical appeals. Even though ecological damage is an almost invariable side-effect of commercialization, the obvious conclusion that the economy of attention must necessarily be embedded in a pertinent ecology has received little notice to date.

This ignorance, as demonstrated in Chapter VI "Social Media and the Ecology of Emotion", becomes irresponsible in the face of the upsurge of those social media whose focus is on user data acquisition. Initially, social media were hailed for democratizing celebrity culture. With social media, the once elitist privilege of working for the wage of fame finds itself socialized. The business model of social media is the idea of scaling the business model of advertisement-financed mass media, such as commercial TV, down to the level of the hawker's tray, thus allowing everybody to participate in the worldwide market (read internet) where information is exchanged for attention. Abolished are the gatekeepers who used to control access to old media. An unexpected effect was that this socialization has been widely taken as a licence for defamation and bullying. In the social exchange of attention, it all too easily happens that groups of participants feel themselves denied the recognition they believe they deserve. On social media platforms, resentment, the self-help of starving self-esteem, encounters unprecedented opportunities for taking revenge. Since resentment must find like-minded followers in order to thrive, media dispensing with gatekeepers provide an ideal platform for resentment in search of entourage. Since it is so easy in social media to find fealty in resentment, aggressive insults, denouncement and disinformation prove to be capable strategies for attracting attention, paid in currencies such as clicks, dwell times, follows and likes.

In recent years a wave of resentment driven politicking has swept the internet. The toxic underbelly of social media platforms, where emotionalized hypes and, in particular, negative emotions spread as freely as climate pollutants, has been laid bare. We now face an emotional climate change, a warm-up of the mental sphere: verily the economy of attention is catching up with money economy in conjuring up an ecological problem. The ecology in which the economy of attention is embedded is the stock of trust and benevolence presupposed and maintained by the members of society in their everyday dealings. This stock is the epitome of an ecological resource. It is of vital significance for the overall quality of life attainable in society, it is indivisible, which means that it is of the nature of a *commons*. A commons is a resource usable by everybody though subject to the condition of sustainability: its consumption must not outstrip its regeneration. Since nobody can be excluded from its use, self-interested users have no disincentive to exploiting it without contributing to regeneration. This way ecological resources are run down. Users who make resentment a strategy to collect attention follow the path of exploiting, i.e. pollute, the social commons while shirking payment for the damage. This way, the emotional climate change is brought about.

Under conditions such as these, there are only two ways of preventing ecological disaster: limiting access to the commons by government intervention, or overcoming the perverse incentive to such ecological damage through ethical conviction. In the case of the social commons, limiting access by official regulation means censorship;

this, however, is yet another way of damaging the stock of trust and benevolence incorporated in the citizens' psyches. The only remaining option of ecological policy thus points to ethical persuasion, which, in turn, is hopeless as long as it relies on appeals to duty or promises of otherworldly reward.

Emotional pollution, which might be the darkest side of the success story of vanity fairs, is what an ethics tailored to a society making substantial use of vanity fairs must deal with. Chapter VII "Moral Elegance: An Ethics Tailored to Vanity Fairs?" returns to the moral handicap of vanity. It closes this treatise by devising a secular ethics that does not decry the craving for attention, but rather suggests utilizing the pains we take regarding our role in the consciousness of others as a positive force, using it to bridge the motivational gap between the individual pursuit of interest and the promotion of the common good.

References

Bataille, Georges. 1967. *The Accursed Share*, vol. 1, translated from French by Robert Hurley, New York: Zone Books.

Chalmers, David J. 2000. What is a Neural Correlate of Consciousness? In *Neural Correlates of Consciousness*, ed. Thomas Metzinger, 17–39. Cambridge: MIT Press.

Davenport, Thomas H., and John C. Beck. 2001. *The Attention Economy. Understanding the New Currency of Business*. Boston: Harvard Business School Press.

Davidson, Donald. 1974. *On the Very Idea of a Conceptual Scheme: Inquiries into Truth and Interpretation*. Oxford: Clarendon Press.

Dennett, Daniel C. 1994, September 1–3. Consciousness in Human and Robot Minds. In *IIAS Symposium on Cognition, Computation and Consciousness, Kyoto*; online http://ase.tufts.edu/cogstud/dennett/papers/concrobt.htm.

Falkinger, Josef. 2005, March. Limited Attention as the Scarce Resource in an Information-Rich Society, IZA Discussion Paper No. 1538.

Franck, Georg. 1989, August. Die neue Währung: Aufmerksamkeit. Zum Einfluss der Hochtechnik auf Zeit und Geld (The new Currency: Attention. On the Influence of High Technology on Time and Money). *Merkur 486*: 688–701.

Franck, Georg. 1998. *Die Ökonomie der Aufmerksamkeit* (The Economy of Attention). Munich: Carl Hanser Verlag

Franck, Georg. 1993, September/October/2018. The economy of attention (English translation of "Ökonomie der Aufmerksamkeit". *Merkur 534/535*: 748–761, translated by Silvia Plaza and Robert van Krieken, *Journal of Sociology 55* (1), 2018, pp. 8–19.

Goldhaber, Michael. 1997. The economy of attention and the Net. *First Monday, 2* (4), 7 Apr 1997.

James, William. 1890. *The Principles of Psychology*. New York: Henry Holt.

Lasch, Christopher 1979. *The Culture of Narcissism*. London: Abacus.

Mauss, Marcel. 1925. *The Gift*, translated from French by Jane I. Guyer, Chicago: Hau Books.

Nagel, Thomas. 1974. What is it Like to be a Bat? *Philosophical Review* 83: 181–195.

Pashler, Harold. 1998. *The Psychology of Attention*. Cambridge, MA: MIT Press.

Pylkkänen, Paavo. 2014. Can Quantum Analogies Help us to Understand the Process of Thought? *Mind and Matter* 12 (1): 61–91.

Rizzolatti, Giacomo., and Laila, Craighero. 2004. The mirror-neuron system. *Annual Review of Neuroscience* 27 (1): 169–192.

Samuelson, Paul A. 1947. *Foundations of Economic Analysis*. Cambridge, Massachusetts: Harvard University Press.

Simon, Herbert A. 1971. Designing Organisations for an Information-Rich World. In *Computers, Communications and the Public Interest*, ed. M. Greenberger, 38–52. Baltimore: Johns Hopkins Press.

I Competition in the Service of Self-esteem

The most obvious social manifestations of the unspoken passion called vanity are elegance and fashion. Elegance and fashion concern our obsession with outward appearance. Even though the goodness referred to by ‘looking good’ is a matter of individual taste, elegance and fashion are eminently social phenomena. Looking good according to one’s individual taste cannot be separated from one’s feeling attractive, which, in turn, cannot be separated from finding oneself involved in a competition for attention. Vanity thus makes public appearance in the form of attractiveness contests or, put more succinctly, vanity fairs.

Seemingly, elegance and fashion are mere luxuries. In fact, appearance is all that matters; substance is immaterial. Elegance and fashion, accordingly, hold dubious value to the honestly down-to-earth. Since relying on nothing but individual taste, they seem to resist an objective way to be measured. Remarkably, though, they do not resist measurement altogether. They prove powerful in mobilizing preparedness to pay, which is a measuring rod, to be sure. Needless to say, this power renders the cult around attractiveness all the more scandalous to those of a substance-minded orientation. Nevertheless, the scandal proves a constant when we look back through history. As old as moral instruction is as a literary genre, so old is the vanity fair as a literary trope. As old as the moral preached, however, so old is the futility of the preaching. Vanity is as immune to education programmes as is eroticism.

In order to translate this individual obsession into the context of the market economy, aspects susceptible to quantification have to be accounted for. Such an aspect, for example, would be the turnover of the industries that supply the goods that vanity demands. It would be extremely interesting to know this percentage in order to determine the extent of the preparedness to pay for the goods. Regrettably, it is hopeless to measure the turnover that is due to vanity goods. It would require sorting out gilded or conspicuous[1] consumption from consumption in general. Gilded consumption implies buying things that are not necessary, but that make people take notice. It is, to put it differently, consumption in the service of attractiveness. The reason why it is hopeless to sort out this segment of consumption is not only that the borders are

[1] This term is, as is well known to Veblen (1899).

G. Franck, *Vanity Fairs*,
https://doi.org/10.1007/978-3-030-41532-7_2

blurred—but, above all, that it will be hard to find any consumption not infected by the intention to impress. In affluent societies, it would be the purchases only by the really poor that could lay bare impression-free consumption. In this respect we can at least discern the larger part of consumer goods to be in the service of attractiveness.

The Economy of Self-esteem

What, accordingly, is the rationale behind this predominant motive to spend in excess of basic needs? Just vanity? The problem may seem that vanity is the wrong word to explain the phenomenon, because the word suggests more than excessive self-regard and overblown pride. It also conveys the notion of a well-developed appetite for attention, hence the propensity to compete for its receipt. Self-regard and overblown pride cannot be separated from caring about what other people think of us. By including this phenomenon of caring about what other people think of us, vanity turns out to be the right word for this self-gratifying motive of spending.

The propensity to compete for attention, however, clearly exceeds mere caring about one's outer appearance. It includes the general concern about what others think of us. Vanity, in this regard, says something fundamental about what it means to be human. Humans are beings conscious of themselves and, in addition, social creatures. It is this kind of self-awareness we share with our closest relatives in the animal kingdom. It is such that we are not only aware of our fellow humans, but also of being paid attention by them—that is, we are aware of playing a role in the minds of others.[2] And we are social animals like our animal relatives in the sense that our main business consists in observing one another and communicating with one another, i.e. in exchanging attention with our conspecifics.

We are naturally born attention addicts. Our psyche will be permanently injured if it does not receive a certain minimum of attention. Total withdrawal of attention can be lethal. Babies die from lack of attention; adults experience solitary confinement

[2]According to an influential theory going back to George Herbert Mead, the American founder of social psychology, the phylogenesis of self-awareness originated in an emergent awareness of the symmetry of the exchange of attention among social animals (Mead 1934). When paying attention to you, my interest is not only in your outer behaviour, but also in looking for signs of whether you pay attention to me. When realizing that you pay attention to me, I implicitly become aware of the other mind. This awareness is common knowledge in the animal kingdom. The decisive step to explicit self-awareness lies in performing the symmetry of the attention exchanged in one's own consciousness. If I pay attention to your paying attention to me, accomplishing this symmetry is the decisive step in my overtaking of your perspective on me. This overtaking, Mead suggests, does not presuppose linguistic means of representation. It might explain, rather, how self-awareness emerged in more highly-developed animal consciousness. By thus overtaking the other's perspective on oneself as one's own perspective onto oneself, the evaluative trait of the view is absorbed along with it. When paying attention to you, my attention is always charged with feelings: either I like you or I detest you, either I admire you or I am filled with contempt for you, I feel myself either to be superior or inferior to you. My view regarding myself, accordingly, is either positive or negative. Hence the affective trait of self-awareness.

as torture. Our psyche needs attention paid by other psyches in the same way as our bodies need endorphins.

The attention we pay to one another tends to be charged with feelings. With feelings of sympathy or antipathy, respect or condescension, admiration or contempt, friendliness or hostility, and so on. By virtue of having emerged from the awareness of being paid attention, human self-awareness is far from being the purely cognitive affair of the *Know thyself!* type, as routinely dealt with in the philosophical seminar. The self-reference of the consciousness that is aware of being paid attention is itself charged with feelings of esteem or blame. It is the consciousness not primarily of an 'I' in the function of the (Kantian) 'I think' that must accompany any representation, but of an 'ego' whose prime concern is the appreciation it feels entitled to. The self-awareness of the ego includes an essentially affective quality that 'cold' cognition about the self does not (cf. Leary et al. 1995, p. 519). In order to understand our longing for appreciative attention, we thus have to inquire into *affective self-awareness*, the sensitivity of the ego that feels good or bad depending on its answer to the question: how do I stand in front of myself? Am I entitled to like myself or am I bound to feel contempt toward myself when applying the scales of appreciation I apply to others? Am I, according to the standards I apply to others, entitled to be proud? Or should I rather be ashamed?

Compared to self-knowledge, self-valuation would be a simple and straightforward affair if it consisted of nothing more than valuation according to one's own standards. One's judgment of self-esteem would then be autonomous. In fact, however, we are far from autonomous in determining our self-esteem. Even though our own judgment does matter, it is subject to *social proof*. What we are allowed to think of ourselves is contingent on what others think of us. The ego's concern of self-esteem is far from being self-centred only. It is both resolutely selfish *and* eminently social. The ego must earn its living by getting attention. In order to grow, its income of attention has to grow. To increase this income, it has to raise the preparedness to pay on the part of its fellows. This preparedness depends on what you can offer in exchange. Since your own expenditure reacts to what others offer, it is clear that there is something like a symmetry between taking and paying in this exchange. We are dependent on others as others depend on us. The egos are nodes in a net of interdependency. As pointed out above, it makes no sense to isolate the ego from its social context. The ego, rather, embodies the social context. This is what precludes affective self-awareness from being a comparably simple and straightforward affair. It includes nothing less than the social economy of attention.

Nevertheless, inclusion does not amount to merger. Though dependent on income, the ego's opinion of itself is no mere reflex of the payroll. In self-esteem, the ego's valuation also refers immediately to itself. When wondering how I should evaluate myself, *unmediated self-respect* is the first consideration. The first question therefore becomes whether I feel worthy of the adulation with which I am showered. If immediate self-respect says no, applause is not worth much. Even admiration, one of the highest qualities of esteem, is devalued if coming from quarters I myself do not respect. Due to the voice of unmediated self-respect, the attention received finds itself not only tallied as revenue, but assessed also in terms of quality by the receiver. The worth of the attention income, to reiterate, depends on both the feelings it transports and on the estimation that the receiver has for the sender.

In contrast to self-esteem, unmediated self-respect has a legitimate claim to autonomy. That claim rests on the independence and stability of self-respect and on whether I am helplessly delivered to the vicissitudes of social interaction or strong enough to endure disappointments and setbacks. Frustration is inevitable in the procurement of attention. To prevent breakdown after every setback, the ego has to acquire a certain autonomy, an autonomy whose classical analogy is of the individual household embedded in the social economy. This autonomy cannot be other than conditional, to be sure. It makes no sense to isolate the household from the social economy. Though relative, the autonomy of the household is crucial with regard to the value attached to the payments received.

It is up to the receiver to factor in the esteem held for the sender. The metaphor of the household should prove helpful, thus, for addressing the entity that performs the assessment of income while converting it into the asset of self-worth. It should even make sense to talk of an accounting system for highlighting the sub-system that handles the conversion of the flow of income into an asset.

To summarize: self-worth as an asset relies on a dualism of jurisdiction: on *unmediated self-respect* on the one hand and *mediated self-esteem* on the other. Unmediated self-respect is what carries out the evaluation of attention income and gauges the esteem the ego deserves according to the scales it applies in its appreciation of others. Self-respect is where morality enters affective self-awareness. The strength of unmediated self-respect is what the uprightness of character depends on. Mediated self-esteem, in contrast, accounts for the fact that what we are allowed to think of ourselves does not depend on our own judgment only, but also on what others think of us. Hence, the self-esteem we can afford is measured by our own standards of value judgment as well as by the estimation we receive from our fellow humans. Affective self-awareness differs from cognitive self-awareness both in its evaluative character and in the involvement of other people's attention.

Tricks of Creative Accounting in the Economy of Self-esteem

In a sense, the very dependency of self-esteem on other people's judgment amounts to a narcissistic injury. We are not masters of our self-esteem. And yet in another sense, this dependency provides a gift of opportunities that in other circumstances would be deemed fantastic. It means that the ego has an unlimited potential to grow. Provided unmediated self-respect does not discredit the attention received, the ego can grow as long as its income of appreciative attention grows. The narcissistic injury meets an antidote—it is compensated by the almost unlimited self-enhancement opportunities the dependency engenders. Why be upset by the loss of autonomy if it allows you to pamper the ego? The compensation, of course, looks somewhat dubious; the gift smacks of poison. The opportunity of self-enrichment offers an invitation to opportunistic and strategic behaviour in social exchange. There is a wide range of crooked and downright fraudulent methods of gathering up attention. Children throw their weight around, juveniles show off, adults befriend others whose only merit is that they are flatterers. The corrupting force inherent in the desire to enrich oneself with attention is what necessitates the description of vanity as a vice—if not as a mortal sin, as the catechism decrees.

Yet the pursuit of attention cannot be a vice as such. Humans are naturally born attention addicts. We are well advised, therefore, to draw a line between the morally admissible and morally inadmissible in this pursuit. Drawing this line is not so easy, to be sure. It proves feasible, nevertheless, by invoking the aforementioned household metaphor. For the household—that is to say for the individual member of the social economy—the invitation to self-enrichment connotes the reinforcement of the pursuit of attention. Since the growth of the ego knows no limits from within, the appetite for attention knows no saturation. Instead, there is an excessive demand that puts pressure on the internal working of the household. The pressure is on utilizing the degrees of freedom controlled by unmediated self-respect. Even though it would be pointless to escape social proof, there is leeway in the assessment of the attention revenue und in its conversion into self-esteem. In terms of accounting you can raise the book value of a given quantity of attention by way of manipulating the esteem you have for the sender according to their preparedness to praise you. Raise your appreciation of those who flatter you and lower it for those who are critical or refusing, and you find the book value of the income your ego so desperately needs increased. All that is required for this whimsical kind of value creation is that unmediated self-respect turns a blind eye to the doubling of standards. The difference between the morally admissible and morally inadmissible in the pursuit of self-esteem lies in the objectivity of one's evaluation of the source of praise received. The morally admissible evaluation occurs when one perceives the attention given in a true light. The morally inadmissible evaluation is that which deliberately misconstrues the esteem for the sender.

It would be sheer hypocrisy to condemn our propensity for adapting the esteem we have for others to the esteem they show to us. Nor are compliments as such to be deemed a vice. There is no falling in love without making beautiful eyes, nor is there true friendship without partisan praise. The border between complacency and corruption is always negotiable. Thus we are navigating mined terrain. The household metaphor, nevertheless, provides the means for drawing a line in this uncertain territory. It is the distinction between correct and false accounting. This distinction, again, is at the mercy of lawyers' scrutiny, but it is clear in virtue of its own logic.

Nothing more, in turn, is required for turning vanity into a vice than allowing the esteem held for others to resort to double standards. It depends, in consequence, on the steadfastness of unmediated self-respect as to whether vanity plays fair or foul. The reason for being steadfast is not only mere formal correctness. The problem with vanity's strategy of self-enhancement is that it builds on self-deception. The trick behind this foul play lies in undercutting unmediated self-respect. Since self-respect has a say in the determination of self-esteem, undercutting its voice means to compromise self-esteem as such. That self-esteem which is acquired by undercutting self-respect is of a baser metal. It may take the form of megalomania, but in any case it corrupts the individual character's uprightness. It is easily recognized in the exchange by the disproportion between the receptivity in taking and the reluctance in returning attention.

Vanity is a reaction to pressure felt from within. It is driven by an aspiration for self-esteem that exceeds the fund of praise others are prepared to grant. This thirst for attention is as susceptible to internal manipulation as is the appreciation the ego is willing to bestow on others. In this regard, the pressure to which vanity is a reaction is not all too serious. There are other, considerable threats, however. They come about when indispensable acknowledgement is withheld. There is a minimum of acknowledgement one requires to keep self-esteem intact. And there are situations where refusal of recognition even delivers blows to self-respect. Think of the situation of being betrayed publicly by a person you are in love with, or being denied respect by a person you have hitherto trusted unconditionally. For situations such as these, the economy of self-esteem keeps in reserve a kind of self-help: we instinctively get huffy and start to persuade ourselves and others that those withholding what we so desperately need are themselves not worthy of respect. By thus devaluating the good we think we cannot forego, it feels easier to bear the withdrawal. To put it differently: *resentment is a proven painkiller for injured self-esteem.*

Resentment differs from vanity in that it is a defence mechanism in reaction to external disappointment. As a reflex of self-help, it tends to be more instinctive than vanity's deliberate opportunism. Its way of manipulating evaluation of the other person is derogatory, whereas vanity tends to adulation. The transition between the two is fluid, however. Vanity also resorts to derogation when reacting to criticism and disdain. The negative impact of disapproval can also be reduced by answering the offence with disparagement of the offender. Hence, the difference between resentment and vanity's opportunism is a matter of degree.

Resentment, accordingly, is far from being merely an antidote for cases of greatest trouble and distress. It is equally a proven pain-reliever for milder forms of dissatisfaction. It is a strategy readily at hand for dealing with the frequent disappointments in the social exchange of attention. Due to the constant excess demand for attention, it is very easy to feel denied the recognition one considers oneself to deserve. Shot through as it is with temptations to excessiveness, the pursuit of attention is plagued with occasions of disappointment as a result. Only a slight curbing of the control exerted by self-respect turns the attention longed-for but not gained into proverbial sour grapes. No wonder, thus, that resentment is such a rich, bubbling source of everyday malice.

In the economy of attention, there are even markets for sour grapes. There are markets for services of denigration and defamation that serve effective demand. Effective demand means preparedness to pay for the item supplied. In order to turn the recognition one desperately longs for but feels denied into sour grapes, one has to persuade not only oneself, but others also that those deemed offenders are themselves not worthy of respect. Growing sour grapes is thus contingent on the need to find consensus. It is only by finding consensus that the strategy really works. Unless followers are found, resentment degenerates into personal embitterment. In that situation, the denigrator finds himself back to square one. He still faces the task of earning attention. What has changed in his quest for consensus is just the target group. The new target group is those who themselves are in the business of denigration. Since the business includes the task of finding followers, the new target group tends to offer particularly fertile ground for conscription of new acolytes. It includes all those who themselves suffer injury to their self-esteem to even a minor degree. It includes all those whose resentment expresses itself in the preparedness to pay attention to whatever endorses their sense of injury. It includes, to put it bluntly, the demand for news, rumours, half-truths, conspiracy theories and eventually plain lies—if only they confirm the slanderer's prejudice.

Sour grapes are 'goods' turned into 'bads', so to speak, which nevertheless meet effective demand for some kind of consoling salve. Since the effectiveness of demand depends not only on the individuals' preparedness to pay, but also on the effort it takes to get access to the market and to find partners for exchange, changes of the form of the market for sour grapes promise to be of some relevance for the role that resentment can play in the mental sphere. We will necessarily return to the topic therefore in the context of social media. For the moment, however, we should stay focused on deepening the understanding of vanity fairs as collective expressions of the interaction of individual households of self-esteem.

The Upward Bias of the Valuation of Attention Income

Our account of vanity is still incomplete. There is a borderline case of adaptive valuation of incoming attention which, though acting like creative accounting, happens without deliberate manipulation. The fact that self-esteem is contingent on social proof is also consequential for our estimation of others. Since the power of proof does not depend on whether it concerns self-esteem or the esteem others deserve, it is only logical that we transfer it accordingly. We are not indifferent, that is, to the attention payers receive from third parties. Those who are paid ample attention from their surroundings rise in our respect without having to make any conscious effort. Any attention we may receive from them thus enjoys a corresponding rise. This value will therefore increase all the more the higher the income the sender earns in sum, i.e. in society. This means that the value of attention received comes as a function of the wealth the sender is known for. We tend, all things being equal, to prefer attention from attention-rich quarters to attention from attention-poor. Doesn't this preference, though working entirely sub-consciously, border on applying double standards?

At first glance, the weighting of attention according to the earnings of the payer seems to be correct with regard to accounting. It matters whether one is recognized by someone who is well known or by just anybody. Playing a role in the consciousness of someone who is well known is of two-fold advantage. First, it allows one's self-esteem to participate in the renown of the owner; second, it augments one's own prestige in the eyes of third persons who pay attention to the social dealings of others. It can even be read as a sign of accuracy and fine-tuning of the accounting system that converts income into self-esteem that it is highly sensitive to kudos, reputation, renown, prestige, prominence and fame—that is, to the various forms that the wealth of attention assumes.

In a sense, of course, it is. The income that is converted internally into self-esteem is converted externally—i.e. in the perspective of third persons who register the attention income from outside—into kudos, prestige, renown, prominence etc. These forms of wealth are constitutive of social status, as are material wealth and endowments of power. They are socially objective and result from a selection process that brings to light the preparedness to pay attention among the population at large. They also give expression to the fact that the economy of attention is a market economy that connects exchange with the valuation of the goods exchanged. Insofar as it makes no sense to isolate the individual receiver from the social economy of attention, it is pointless to blame the receiver for taking the socially established prices into account. Looked at from a slightly different angle, it is perverse to attach prices to attention. Attention is not merchandise in the first place, but the capacity of conscious experience. This capacity lies at the foundations of our very humanity. When exchanging attention interpersonally we give active expression to our conviction that we, as humans, share this capacity even though we have no immediate access to and thus no tangible evidence of other consciousness. This raises the question of whether pricing this invaluable good might amount to a pricing of persons.

The problem with such humanistic reservations is that they do not offer a cure for the widespread fascination that prestige, prominence, fame, etc. exert. It is hard to be totally unimpressed by the enormity of attention a person is capable of attracting. People pay attention not only to one another, but also to what others pay to third parties. In the same sense as we individually tally recognizing attention as an endorsement of self-esteem, we collectively interpret the social distribution of attention as a measure of the worthiness of interest in particular people. If someone is well known or even well known for being known, there is a tendency to turn the crowd of attention directed at this person into an aura that surrounds her or him. It takes deliberate effort to brush the transfiguring glow away.

Indulging in the fascination, we find ourselves discriminating between attention that is of attention rich and attention that is of attention poor origin. This discrimination, though probably not even intended, is suspiciously close to that between flatterers and critics. The drive behind it is the same: vanity. The ego discriminates according to the impact the banked attention has upon its self-esteem. Small wonder that vanity is obsessed with boasting about attention won from celebrities.

Vanity, accordingly, is one of the major supports of social hierarchy. It favours those in the upper ranks of society and discriminates against those in the lower ranks. And it does so with a force not exerted by outer authority. The force exerted by vanity relies on our inner economy. It is exercised in virtue of our own autonomy in assessing the quality of a given quantity of earned attention. The assessment, if not manipulated on purpose or made deliberately oblivious to discrimination, works routinely in a subconscious mode. Its evolution most probably predates human culture. It is an inclination deserving to be called instinctive, since it is observed even in the animal kingdom. In the wolf pack and in the monkey troop, the chief is that one alpha animal that requires payment of attention by all others, but who himself need not pay respect to anybody. He who is respected as the richest in terms of attention is not only entitled to dominate the community, but expected to discriminate according to status. The miserable creatures at the bottom of the hierarchy are those having to pay attention to everybody but being paid respect by nobody. The social hierarchy, to put it differently, is negotiated in the exchange of attention instead of being fought by brute violence (which would be detrimental to the group's fitness for survival). Brute violence is used only to break ties. Accounting for a person's wealth of attention is a means, thus, and may be the most basic means worth its name, of establishing a social gradient. Even if you may think that we should overcome this atavistic inclination, it would be naïve, if not downright ignorant, to disregard this widespread inclination, which deserves to be called a kind of instinctive snobbery.

It may go too far to claim that we are a species of naturally born snobs. Snobbery is more than the inclination to discriminate according to social rank. It is the obsession with eroticizing of the social gradient (as pointed out in Adorno 1958/1991). Yet, even this obsession is deeply ingrained in the intra-psychic economy of self-esteem. And it reveals, by way of exaggeration, how the intra-psychic economy of self-worth embodies the social economy of attention. Social rank, to be sure, is external to what the individual does in assessing and converting its income of attention into the asset of self-esteem. Yet, this externality finds itself internalized in the individual's accounting of the worth of the attention received.

If not naturally born snobs, we are naturally born slaves of vanity. We suffer from self-subjugation under the yoke of mediated self-esteem. It is by nature, to be sure, that we fell into this way of life. But does that mean that we are once and for all unable to alter it? Are there no strategies, to be learned from whatever culture, of emancipation from this state of nature, of liberating ourselves from the obsession with what other people think of us? Why let society decide for us what is worthy of attention? What is this dependency good for after all?

Congenital addiction to attention appears to be profound. However, exceptions to this addiction can be found in cultures of spirituality throughout the world. Characteristic of these cultures are the hermits and ascetics who forswear the need for attention. Their answer to this narcissistic need lies in overcoming narcissism altogether. This alternative is intriguing and worth serious consideration.

In order to take the suggestion seriously we again have to keep unmediated self-respect and mediated self-esteem apart. It is conceivable, given the evidence of those hermits and ascetics, to overcome the dependency on the attention of our fellow humans. Yet, it is hardly conceivable that the self can do without unmediated self-respect as long as it is aware of itself. Self-awareness includes the capability of applying value judgment to oneself. Dismissing mediated self-esteem means to dismiss social proof of self-evaluation, i.e. to monopolize immediate self-respect. There is ample evidence that hermits and ascetics do not forswear self-respect. They, of course, pursue the highest possible moral standards. They teach their disciples to dispense with mediated self-esteem and instead to focus, without distraction, on realizing one's spiritual nature. Their doctrine of salvation is to forget our being involved in the social economy of attention, thus preparing one's inner life for higher grades of autonomy.

Yet, this liberation from vanity comes at a price. Apart from extraordinary strength and endurance, the therapy requires self-esteem to stand on one leg. From a yogi standpoint, this may not be asking too much. In ordinary people like you and I, the requirement to uphold self-esteem alone might overstrain immediate self-respect. A characteristic aberration symptomatic of this one-sided support is moral haughtiness, the compensation for the painful renunciation by overblown pride of one's moral excellence. Moral haughtiness is a bad alternative to vicious vanity and equally repugnant. It all too easily reveals a frustrated longing for recognition.

The threat of moral haughtiness, nevertheless, is a minor setback compared to the loss of inter-subjectivity which occurs when shutting down the dependent department of self-esteem. Exposing one's opinion of oneself to social proof gives rise to a tireless motivation for caring about the role one plays in other minds. It turns interest in one's fellow humans' thinking into a main concern of self-interest, thus fuelling the development of human inter-subjectivity to unprecedented levels of sophistication. Mediated self-esteem is the motive behind the sophistication of manners, speech, posture, gesture and body language, all of which involuntarily give expression to inner life. In order to develop pleasant manners, witty speech, dignified posture and body language proficiency you have to train your empathetic sensorium, including your 'theory of other minds', i.e. your capability to infer from the behaviour you observe what goes on in the other psyche. In psychology, this capability is rightly called 'theory of mind', since its acquisition includes rehearsing the role one wants to play in other people's consciousness. In a society whose members have given up the incentive of self-esteem, the cultivation or even minding of these capabilities might turn into a mere luxury, if not a full-blown, frivolous pursuit. Small wonder that the concern for these capabilities features as epitome of devilish temptation in so many of the ancient legends of hermits and ascetics.

The devil is in the detail. It is not without reason, of course, that being concerned about the role one plays in the consciousness of others is suspected to detract from the mindful care of one's own soul. To that extent, spirituality has good reason to fight the addiction to attention. On the other hand, is there anything better suited to making us aware that our fellow humans are embodied souls like ourselves than our caring about the role we play in their consciousness? We are addicted to attention not because we are enchanted by the idea of our personal data being processed by the neural machinery of a biological computer, but by the idea of being welcomed by someone else who feels themselves to *be* an experiencing subject that endows its attention with feelings. Even those who make the intellectual presumption that there is no such thing as a soul pay homage in deeds to it when feeding their ego. This involuntary if tacit recognition of our conscious, subjectively experiencing nature is what first turns us into members of a truly human society. Overcoming the pursuit of attention would mean abolishing the strongest motive for dealing with one another as embodied souls, i.e. as true humans.

Vanity is an intriguing alloy of vice and virtue. You cannot have one without the other. The dependent nature of self-esteem has the double effect of raising, on the one hand, inter-subjectivity to the heights of its possibilities and, on the other hand, of subtly corroborating social inequality. By virtue of the connection between self-esteem and received esteem, self-regard finds itself coupled to empathy. It pays to pay attention to the attention others pay. Isn't it in this way that we are first turned into pleasant people? Nevertheless, by paying attention to what others pay attention to we find ourselves lured into favouring those who are richly paid. And we have good reason to care for being paid attention by those who are rich in attention. The attention from those rich in attention is impregnated with the attention they have managed to attract: it carries with it something like a certificate of socially-audited premium value. In the exchange of attention, we thus find an inbuilt bias favouring the already better-off at the expense of those receiving little attention. From a strictly egalitarian standpoint this bias looks like a design flaw in the very constitution of affective self-awareness.

Emphasizing the humanistic endowment of our emotionality with vanity is not to play down dehumanizing collateral damage. It means, rather, to take humanism as that which Kant called 'the crooked timber of humanity' (Kant 1784). It induces us to recognize the at once stimulating and controlling function that vanity fairs assume in the cultural sector, without losing sight of the regrettable fact that all higher culture builds on privilege and thus on social injustice. The upward bias in the valuation of attention engenders inequality even where privileges imposed by power relations are absent. And it is even harder to fight than the false accounting of vanity and resentment. It is prone to reinforce nature's unequal distribution of gifts and talents by way of flawless accounting. And the bias promises to grow in impact the heavier the use of vanity fairs by society and the greater the inequality in the social distribution of attention grow.

References

Adorno, Theodor W. 1958/1991. Short Commentaries on Proust. In *idem, Notes to Literature*, vol. 1. Trans. by Shierry Weber Nicholson, 174–184. New York: Columbia University Press (originally published as: Kleine Proust-Kommentare, in: Akzente, 1958, no. 6, pp. 564ff).

Kant, Immanuel. 1784. Idea for a Universal History with a Cosmopolitan Purpose. In Reiss, H. S., Kant. *Cambridge Texts in the History of Political Thought*, 41–53, 2nd ed, eds. H.S. Reiss, and Kant. Cambridge: Cambridge University Press.

Leary, Mark R., Ellen S. Tambor, Sonja K. Terdal, and Deborah L. Downs. 1995. Self-esteem as an Interpersonal Monitor: The Sociometer Hypothesis. *Journal of Personality and Social Psychology* 68 (3): 518–530.

Mead, George Herbert. 1934. *Mind, self, and society*. Chicago & London: Chicago University Press.

Veblen, Thorstein. 1899. *The Theory of the Leisure Class: An Economic Study of Institutions. Introduction by Stuart Chase*. New York: The Modern Library, 1934.

II The Emergence of Canons

A source of energy as fertile and inexhaustible as the craving for self-esteem proves to be should find its way into social uses beyond fashion, amusement and beauty contests. Or, put differently, vanity fairs should be expected wherever strong incentives are required for creating supply intended to meet extraordinarily fastidious demand. In order to set the stage for the inquiry of the role that vanity fairs play in society at large, it might be appropriate thus to inquire about how competitions are dictated by the highest demands of society. How does one determine the highest demand? A task of highest demand is one whose very completion is uncertain. There are various seemingly unsolvable tasks of this sort. Yet the number of such tasks reduces considerably when the solution has to be brought about by competitions for attention.

A field where competitions for attention play a natural role is the market of ideas. The market of ideas has clearly demarcated submarkets: art and science. Both art and science suffer from a disparity between high claims of quality and shaky means of measuring the quality. Let us thus take seriously the claim that the characteristics that make artistic quality and scientific value so particular also make them incommensurable with well-established scales of value. There is nothing like a gold standard applicable to artistic quality or scientific value. There is, nevertheless, a clear-cut selection of works, called the canon, which are supposed to conform to the highest standards. The question is thus: who or what is responsible for the establishment of the canon?

In both art history and the theory of science, the question meets a certain reluctance. The frank answer would have to be that the selection is made by some sort of self-appointed jury. Yet self-appointment is without social control and 'legitimation through procedures', and thus unsuitable for producing binding validity. In order to avoid accusations of outright kingmaking, the selection process is termed a 'discourse'. Discourses are arenas where experts exchange arguments; to establish selections by way of discourse the experts have to reach consensus. Yet a logical fallacy lies at the heart of the invocation of such discourses: it is hopeless to expect that consensus will ever be achieved by such a means, for as long as they exchange arguments, experts will never be in agreement. There are no generally agreed upon

G. Franck, *Vanity Fairs*,
https://doi.org/10.1007/978-3-030-41532-7_3

scales of artistic and scientific value, nor are there chairmen in the self-appointed juries who could enforce decisions (for example by majority rule).

It might be not without reason, consequently, to suspect that the measuring problem of artistic and scientific value is without a solution as long as consensus among the pertaining experts is required. This kind of problem—which clamours to be solved even while we are seemingly ignorant of where to look for the solution—is precisely that which we wish to tackle here.

It may seem frivolous in the eyes of art historians and theorists of science to conjecture that the canons are selected by competitions of the kind of vanity fairs. The suggestion of vanity may require a sense of humour. Nevertheless, it is hard to deny that artists and scientists have laboured since time immemorial for both the wage of money and the wage of fame. They have had to serve two kinds of markets at the same time: markets where goods and services are exchanged for money and markets where expert opinion is given in exchange for interested attention.

Classics Emerge by Way of Career

In the arts, canons are catalogues of classics. Classics do not drop from heaven. A work as finished in the studio is not yet a classic. There may be a classic air about it, but its appearance does not divulge whether it will eventually rise to classic status. The career of a classic depends on more than the work itself. It depends, to begin with, on the attention it receives. Such a career extends over a number of stages. First, the work must make an appearance in the public world: it must be reviewed by experts. Next, it must become generally known in the scene, and assert itself among a specific audience. If it becomes a common topic of conversation, its career as a prospective classic is assured. The last stage in this career is reached when the candidate work survives a phase of inflationary reproduction: something known by everyone up to the point of surfeit, which yet does not repulse, satisfies the requirements of a classic.

Classic objects of art are living proof that artistic quality cannot be reduced to either novelty or rarity. Classics emerge via growth, consumption, and then progressive decay of novelty value. The stage of inflationary reproduction, however, is critical for the selection of paradigmatic quality—a quality enabling something aged to retain its exemplary power. Rarity, therefore, does not define the classic, either. The question of how classics arise is thus equivalent to looking for a quality that transcends both the lure of novelty and the value of rarity.

The sociologically objective outcome of the selection process determining classical quality is a catalogue of recognized paradigmatic works. We find such a catalogue in every artistic discipline. It is in the course of elaborating their specific catalogues of classical works that the various disciplines define their identities. The catalogues are not static, however; they are open-ended and constantly being rewritten. Yet, at any particular point in time any particular version of a canon is binding and exemplary. The existence of such catalogues means that there is something objective about a work's quality that resists reduction to novelty or rarity.

An Objectification of the Judgment of Taste?

That there is an objective quality beyond novelty or rarity is a controversial assumption. Artistic quality addresses the senses. Sensuous judgment is called taste. Taste is judgment not based on stringent rationale. It can only refer to perceptions, feelings, vague ideas, habits. Even the clearest preference or the sharpest distinction based on taste will always remain subjective.

Granting the non-eliminable subjective character of taste does not mean, however, that it should be considered a random bundle of individual predilections and aversions. Taste, rather, is a judgmental power capable of education and sophistication. Taste is susceptible to education, in terms of the recognition of the scope and finesse of one's predilection, the sensitivity of one's aversions. Sophistication means detecting one's slumbering abilities of discrimination. Taste, when developed, is a kind of intelligence (which we recognize inadvertently when rating bad taste as a kind of stupidity). Of course, individual development of taste does not lead on its own to intersubjective agreement in aesthetic judgment among the educated. It rather tends to become idiosyncratic. The idiosyncrasy, nevertheless, concerns the ranking of artworks, not the context of art as such. The context of art is defined by the kind of research that artistic production consists of. What belongs to art and what does not does not depend on pre-established criteria—but on whether the artwork recognizably explores the intelligence that inheres in sensuality. The senses understand more than reason can grasp. They participate in our unbounded desire for understanding the world around us, longing for meaning and coherence. We cannot but crave coherence and meaningfulness because we ourselves are collections of drives the comprehensive satisfaction of which lies in coherence. All perceiving, feeling, striving and concluding is interconnected and mutually serving. Together, these singular acts form a grandiose chord, merge into one comprehensive intelligence.

This chord, however, is not an inborn default. It can only be found out by some kind of 'eureka!' moment, by the working artist being surprised at finding themself resonating with a stimulus exposed in the stage of the work materializing before one's eyes or ears (or indeed hands, mouth or nose). To put it differently, *artistic production is the great laboratory for the research of those desires of the senses that cannot be recognized but by fulfilment.* This laboratory is what all higher education of taste relies on. Classic works are those which explain this to us—or rather, which make us feel this. Canonical works seem to be motivated to a degree that invariably surpasses our ability to explain. Classic works remain surprising because we do not fully understand the way our senses bring about the impression of overwhelming quality. There is something surprising about classic works, and yet they are demonstrations of attunement down to their minute details. Even the traditional heritage embodied in the succession of canonical works seems to be logical in the sense that each work answers to its predecessor in a surprising, but also surprisingly logical, manner. These works are so evidently convincing that this must have something to do with our own sensuousness and intelligence. When we sense these works' motivation, their form, expression and symbolism commingle and enrich each other, they make us aware of how far our capacity for experiencing can reach. Sensorial motivation, in other words, means that a classic work is exceptionally precise in addressing both the synaesthetic potential of our sensuousness and the subtle needs of our attention.[1]

Conceiving taste as sensuous intelligence does not mean leaving its thoroughly subjective nature behind. It rather seems to suggest that the objective status of artistic quality must be rooted in social convention. Reducing classical quality to convention, however, is tantamount to reducing it to what sociologist Pierre Bourdieu calls legitimate taste, the taste that elitist class culture has developed for the purpose of establishing social distance (Bourdieu 1979/1984). Denouncing high culture as class culture is not outrageous since it points to the sad fact that all higher culture relies on privilege. Denouncing the canon as an instrument for enforcing class rule does not explain, however, the precision and stability of the selection. Convention or class culture is not the basis of substantive objectivity. Convention is, according to David Lewis' elaborated theory (Lewis 1969), the rule by which arbitrariness is transformed into social norm.

Although aesthetic validity tends to be confused with convention and class rule, it would be hard to find something more stable than the corpus of recognized works of art. The very existence of catalogues of canonical works is a demonstration of a kind of objectivity, an objectivity surpassing even that of the corpus of scientific theory. Theories come and go, the catalogue of classics persists. Theories have limited half-lives; works of art once recognized as canonical will most probably remain so. This stability is all the more remarkable given that each catalogue of canonical works—just like the corpus of theories—is subject to constant debate. Since there is no pre-established system of aesthetic order, one is led to suspect that something else comes into play when individual taste and social convention interact—something not explained by the transformation of arbitrariness into convention.

The Market Called Discourse

There is a way of establishing objectivity that does not contradict the reign of subjectivity: the transformation of subjective taste into economic value. The most typical and most common example of transformation of subjective preferences into socially binding values is market price formation. If aesthetic value were determined in an analogous way, taste and convention would not resist becoming objective.

Aesthetic value has something to do with economic price. After all, art markets exist. But everybody claiming to cherish art will insist that a distinction must be made between prices and aesthetic rank within the art world. It is also important to note that the case of the art market does not apply to architecture. What is traded in architecture is not art, but physical structure. The price of buildings is only marginally related to architectural quality, or, if there are conservation codes for buildings of acknowledged quality, the inverse relationship holds. Not even architectural services

[1] For a discussion of the concept of sensorial motivation, see Franck and Franck (2001).

are priced according to aesthetic quality. Pricing of architectural services follows standard price lists calculated on the basis only of building category and estimated building cost.

The art trade is not the only market where artistic value is negotiated. Another market of this type is the one for published opinion on artistic rank. It is only in the latter market where architectural value or worthiness is established—and, of course, it is here that things must be traded if they are to become classics. Price formation in this market is the first stage in the career of a potential classic. When a work of art appears on this market, this is equivalent to its being born in the social system of art.

Opinions are traded in information markets. Yet, the measure of artistic value or worthlessness is not the price of the information itself. Aesthetic rank is determined by quite a different kind of price formation: by the allocation of votes. Crucial for the ranking of a work of art or of an author is the attention paid to their publicized appearance. What counts is the journalistic resonance, the number of reviews, the number of citations; in short, documented expert attention.

Today, the market for published opinion has taken over the function formerly performed by tacit convention. The opinions traded here are not exclusively concerned with current production. Where such markets exist, tradition is at stake too. The catalogues of canonical works are constantly being updated and revised. It is striking how much opinions vary about recent works and how rapidly and clearly consensus grows with increasing temporal distance. Given lack of temporal distance, one is free, for example, to deny that Richard Meier or Richard Rogers are outstanding architects. Someone confessing to simply not understanding what should be so particular about Adolf Loos or Ludwig Mies van der Rohe will be considered to be outing himself as a philistine rather than to be saying something about quality architecture. The bare fact of continuing presence in public discourse gives rise to unquestionable recognition. Ranking stability tends to produce a catalogue of works which are conspicuously important in the sense that doubt tends to automatically disqualify itself.

Changing Rankings Within the Stable Membership Directory of the Catalogue

Self-disqualifying doubt is equivalent to unquestioned recognition. There is no higher measure of social objectivity. We should, however, wonder how this objectivity comes about. Does subjective taste become objective, or should we rather suspect successful manipulation? Is constant attention a safe measure of aesthetic value? Or is it an indication that opinion makers have imposed something upon us?

With regard to our career model of the emergence of classics, the answer is not set in stone. The initial stage the model provides is that the work enters the discourse; it must be published, publicly exhibited, reviewed; it must acquire the status of having *arrived*. Even at this first stage, the workings of the market of published opinion will not always be straightforward. Fraud and manipulation are not unheard of. Artists are built up and significance is hyped. The crucial question is how far the slimy tentacles of fraud and manipulation will reach. Publicity and publication power may get anything across for a short while, but doubt remains as to whether wheeling and dealing, the kindling of pressure, can impose lasting importance to any random work.

The test is distributed over the subsequent stages of the candidate's career. No work has ever become a classic without having become fashionable at some time (though often posthumously). There is no direct ascent from initial reputation to Parnassus. Rather, the attention the work is paid has to grow into outright fame. In order to do so, it will not be enough that those initially interested turn into admirers. The audience paying attention has to grow beyond the fan club of those impressed by the work itself. The work has to become fashionable in the sense that crowds mainly interested in what others pay attention to become intrigued. Becoming fashionable means that the accumulation of attention goes through a phase of self-amplification. The work starts to get paid attention not only for those features which triggered its career in the first place, but for its having moreover managed to become such a big earner of attention. Conspicuous wealth finds itself activated as a capital that starts to be profitable on its own. Only with the help of this self-amplification of attention wealth, can the work become truly famous.

Fame, though needed for elevating a work to the heights of a classic, is not on its own sufficient for performing the task, however. The tentacles of fraud and manipulation may still be in play. Fashions are rarely free of manufactured hype. Hype is functional, nevertheless, for reasons of aesthetic conversion. Aesthetic conversion is an experience well known to us all: we find something novel appearing on the scene to be grating at first; gradually, we begin to take it seriously because of all the commotion around it, and at last we come to appreciate what at first we believed was nonsense. In retrospect we conclude that our first impression was mistaken and that we were converted by experiencing a flash of enlightenment. Like the father who once commented on a work by Picasso that his child could have painted it, who some time later feels the scales fall from his eyes, and whose Damascene conversion is complete when he becomes a grandfather collecting cubist painting.

Fashions in art are mass-pullers for aesthetic conversion. They pose as educators in things aesthetic. They have the effect of expanding the laboratory for sensory experience far beyond the artists' studios. Fashion does this by recruiting test persons in masses for testing a work's capacity to resonate with the public. In this phase of mass conversion, much more attention is mobilized than the exclusive circles of connoisseurs could contribute. And this attention is involved not only by way of savouring the novel qualities of a motivated work, but also by testing implicitly whether the conversion is sustainable. Those whose conversions were simply an act of jumping on the bandwagon start to lose interest.

The career of the potential classic is about to embark on the third stage: inflation. Fashion results not only in self-amplification of wealth of attention, but, by the same dynamics, in the destruction of the wealth itself. Fashion brings about a proliferation of copies, reproductions and imitations, which invariably results in inflation. Inflation means more and more of the same ad nauseam. Those consumers with more sensitive antennae get fed up and find themselves sniffing around for another innovation. The work, having reached this stage, finds itself immersed in an acid bath that aggressively corrodes novelty and rarity value.

Novelty and rarity are the classical dynamos of attraction. They are what fuels publicity campaigns and unleashes the dynamics of self-reinforcement. In this third stage, these attractors are now drained. Even massive amounts of staged prominence will not withstand the litmus test of inflationary reproduction. This test reveals the durability of a quality which can survive the nausea of inflation and transcends manipulated market value. If novelty and rarity are the only qualities that distinguish a work, its career ends when the fashion is over.

The final and decisive stage in the career of a potential classic consists in its resurrection from the acid bath. From whence comes the power for such a resurrection? The work is now historical, its protagonists are old or dead. The interests once having pushed its fashion are debilitated. With the resurrection of an out-of-fashion work, neither much money nor much attention is to be expected. What makes this out-of-fashion work become a classic is the fourth stage—namely, that it still deserves attention. It must be read, visited or performed, discussed again and again; it must become the object of dissertations and anthologies, finally appearing in textbooks and curricula. We might call this stage *the consolidation of attention income.*

In order to revive a stream of attention payment strong enough to pull the out-of-fashion work out of the acid bath, there must be people capable of recognizing a quality over and above novelty and rarity value. It is here that the saying ‘it takes one to know one’ applies—meaning that only those who themselves are artists or themselves have an artistic vein are equipped to recognize the ongoing significance of an artist out of vogue. There must be a capacity in the appraiser for being surprised by a quality one was unaware of until then. This detection, of course, concerns the ‘how it feels’ quality of aesthetic perception.

In order to bring about the resurrection, it is not enough, however, that individual connoisseurs feel intrigued. The newly intrigued sensitivity must find followers. A work’s ascent to Parnassus is inseparable from taste’s education reaching another level of sophistication. The taste thus undergoing education must not be merely idiosyncratic. In order to bring about the resurrection, considerable numbers of lovers of art must feel intrigued—for it is only by proving itself capable of gaining popularity among art aficionados that the work is ready to scale the loftiest heights of widespread acclaim and reverence.

Once it has become a classic it most probably will remain so. The reason, however, is not that there is a kind of ratchet that prevents the reversal of the ascent. Although the canon is constantly worked over, overhauled, revised and rearranged,[2] membership in the directory is close to irreversible. The explanation of this constancy is found in the

[2]Look for instance at the paradigmatic Cinquecento master painters. In the 19th century, Raphael and Titian were rated at the pinnacle, whereas Tintoretto and Caravaggio were secondary, deemed to lack the noble perfection of the former. Today it seems that we are more impressed by Tintoretto’s compositional power-play and by Caravaggio’s dirty realism than by Raphael’s unshakable ideality or Titian’s ennobling sfumato. Nothing, however, has changed in the league they play in as classics.

selection process. The selection process of classics functions indeed as a kind of self-appointed jury, without formal organization, commission, official order, or regulated membership. It works as a multi-level competition for attention that organizes itself. And it works with such precision and reliability that subsequent corrections of the selection are rare exceptions.

References

Bourdieu, Pierre. 1979/1984. *Distinction: A Social Critique of the Judgement of Taste*. Trans. Richard Nice. Cambridge, MA: Harvard University Press.

Franck, Dorothea, and Georg Franck. 2001. *Quality: On the Poetics of Architecture*. English Trans. Qualität. Von der poetischen Kraft der Architektur. Appeared in Merkur, no. 626, June 2001. Translation available under http://www.iemar.tuwien.ac.at/publications.

Lewis, David. 1969. *Convention: A Philosophical Study*. Cambridge, MA: Harvard University Press.

III Scientific Communication: A Vanity Fair?

In early modernity, science underwent a fundamental change. In the textbook theory of science, this change is attributed to methodological innovations such as experimentation à la Bacon and problem analysis à la Descartes. There was a change in social organization, however, which is no less remarkable. The crowd of migrant scholars populating medieval science started to self-organize into what later came to be called an industry. It is to these two developments that modern science owes its sweeping success.

What does industrialization mean? It means division of labour into two tiers. It means, on the micro-level, to break down complex operations into simpler and simpler manipulations in such a way that the single manipulations become susceptible to mechanization. On the macro-level, it means the differentiation of specialized lines of production that produce inputs for other lines of specialized production, which, in turn, are reintegrated through markets that connect exchange with valuation of the output.

Thought Economy

Historically, the industrialization of knowledge production did not follow but rather preceded the industrialization of material production. In terms of scientific production, the breaking down of complex operations into simpler and simpler ones amounts to what René Descartes named the *rational method* (see Descartes' Discours de la methode, 1637). The problems scientific investigation finds itself confronted with are much too complex to be dealt with in their entirety. The bandwidth of our attention, i.e. of our capacity to consciously process information, is incommensurate with the vast overview required for the professional handling of research questions. Before

The ideas of this section were developed in Franck (1999, 2002, 2015). It would be pedantic to refer to these papers in detail.

G. Franck, *Vanity Fairs*,
https://doi.org/10.1007/978-3-030-41532-7_4

being able to deal with scientific questions, the content has to be sequenced, i.e. cast into the form of a description. Description as such is not enough, however. In order to be dealt with operationally, the description of a complex problem has to be broken down into components of manageable size. The rational method, then, is precisely the instruction of how the complex problem can be broken down into simpler and simpler problems, in such a way that the solution of the complex problem can be constituted from the solutions of the simpler ones. Analysis is the decomposition of problems; synthesis is the formulation of solutions via a recomposition of decomposed problems. As with physical labour, the division of cognitive work not only exploits the economies of routinization, but also allows the use of mechanisms. The mechanisms supporting the mind's own mechanics are of a conceptual nature. Analysis entails description. Language itself is the first and most fundamental way of translating complex ideas into a series of simpler components. To cast an idea into the form of language means to break it down into standardized units (words), suited for sequentially passing the bottleneck of simultaneous processing and for repeated use. By concatenating the units according to mechanical (i.e. syntactic) rules, content is sequenced into the form of sentences, which, in turn, can be linked up to form descriptions of any complexity.

Language thus proves to be the basic technology of *thought economy*. It vastly amplifies the weak forces of unarmed attention. It overcomes the narrow limits of the naturally defined capacity of conscious information processing. Language empowers attention to deal, in a controlled way, with ideas whose complexity vastly overburdens the forces of unarmed attention. It was only logical, thus, that science started developing the potential of language in terms of the economy of thought.[1] By applying language onto itself, i.e. by explicitly describing the meaning of words, words are transformed into *concepts*. Concepts are words turned into tools, sharpened by clear demarcation of their meaning. The leverage of language was further enhanced by extending the specification and refinement of concepts through the elaboration of terminologies, which, in turn, paved the way for the definition of artificial languages such as symbolisms, thereby allowing formalization. It was by way of the formalization of language that thought economy could cross the threshold to mechanization. The upshot of formalization is calculation, i.e. the gain of precise information by a purely mechanical manipulation of symbols. Mechanization advanced when mathematics was utilized as a language of description (and when empiricism, accordingly, developed systematic observation into the methodology of measurement). Simultaneous equation systems are capable of turning descriptions into models that work as abstract machines. In terms of the enhancement of efficiency of human labour, theories built from symbolisms such as differential calculus or the chemical symbolism are competitive with the machinery arming physical labour in heavy industry. Abstract machines, moreover, can be turned into concrete machines when translated

[1]It is strange, thus, to find that the theory of science grossly ignores the role that thought economy plays in scientific research. Remarkable exceptions to the rule are the classics Mach (1883) and Husserl (1935). Until today, even psychology, sociology and economics of science feel justified in circumventing the topic.

into algorithms run on digital machinery. By involving digital machinery, mechanization of cognitive labour finds itself extended to automation.[2] Eventually, cognitive labour thus harnesses external sources of energy, as does physical labour in heavy industry.

Progress in science remains poorly understood if seen only as an accumulation of discoveries. Progress in science has always involved progress in *thought economy*. Thought economy concerns the efficiency of the energy used in cognitive labour, i.e. on attention. Thought economy is that part of the economy of attention that deals with attention in its property as a *scarce resource*. In modern science, economizing attention is not restricted to the micro-level of cognitive labour, however. It is continued on the macro-level by differentiating the overall process of knowledge production into specialized lines of production that produce inputs for other lines of specialized production. It is not until the overall process is thus organized as an industry[3] that the advantages of the division of cognitive labour are fully exploited.

The Emergence of Scientific Communication

Taken as such, differentiated lines of knowledge production are much older than modern science. They are called disciplines, and seem to have subdivided the field of systematic research since its beginning. What did not exist in ancient and medieval science, however, was the regular exchange between producers, the exchange we today call *scientific communication*. Since information is power, there is a constant temptation to monopolize it. Why communicate your discovery, why share it with other researchers if you can sell it to some ruler or patron in order to earn your living? Up to the seventeenth century, scholars, even in mathematics and astronomy, were pre-eminently concerned with protecting their claims to priority through secretiveness and mystification (cf. Rescher 1989, p. 34). Only through the emergence of new means of information sharing, such as academies and learned societies with their meetings and published proceedings, could modern science embark on secure and steady growth.

[2]Today, even the borders between theory and experimentation are blurred by the role that simulation models play in e.g. materials science or the study of climate change. See Galison (1996).

[3]To ward off misleading associations with the notion of industry: the way scientific production organizes itself on the macro-level has nothing to do with centrally-owned production facilities or centrally-managed assembly lines. Those working in knowledge production are characteristically both workers and entrepreneurs. Calling the organizational structure an industry is due to the lack of a better term for the formation of specialized lines of production supplying inputs to other lines of specialized production. Thanks to Sarah Spiekermann for warning me of oblique associations.

Modern science relies on experimentation. By performing experiments, science not only adopted a superior means of testing hypotheses but provided entertainment value as well. The meetings of the academies and learned societies could be used for presenting experiments like circus tricks to an audience that was interested in entertainment of a challenging nature. Not everybody, of course, was admitted to the meetings. It was for reasons of the entertainment of noblemen that the academies could acquire considerable funds from early on. The selective admission of noblemen had a decisive side effect. Aristocrats were supposed to observe a code of conduct different from that of ordinary scholars and businessmen. Noblemen were supposed to be free of the temptation to sell tomorrow as their own discovery what they today learned in a scholarly lecture. The scientist, accordingly, did not risk the theft of his right of authorship and priority. As long as there were reliable witnesses around, this risk was minimal even when other researchers were in the audience. Testimony of a noble audience was the first step to what later came to be called *intellectual property*. By publishing your findings in the right place you could acquire intellectual property of it. In particular, the publication in written form of the proceedings of the meetings proved an effective system for the authentication and protection of the endeavours and innovations of the creative scientist (cf. Ravetz 1971, p. 249). Publication puts intellectual property at the disposal of the general public under the sole condition that its processing into the user's intellectual property is credited by *citation*.

The Measurement of Scientific Information

Efficiency, as important as it is on the individual level of work, is just as important on the collective level of cooperation. As an industry, science is no longer the business of isolated persons or research units, but a social organization that combines the work of specialists who collaborate with other specialists in producing inputs for other lines of specialized production. From a collective point of view, it is only through an efficient division of cognitive labour and an efficient exchange of pre-processed information that science can function rationally. There is, however, no centralized agency planning the distribution of talent and effort over the various lines of research. The division and re-integration of scientific work must organize itself.

How does science organize itself? Does it self-organize in a way that allows or even ensures optimality? Or is the self-organization of distributed scientific labour an impediment to overall efficiency? These are the basic questions in considering the *collective rationality* of science. As long as the available talents and efforts go into occupations that are socially suboptimal, resources will be wasted no matter how hard the individual scientist may have been working.

One may object that the measurement of efficiency, as necessary as it may seem for organizing knowledge production rationally, cannot be applied operationally to scientific work. Efficiency concerns the output into which used resources are transformed. The output of scientific work consists of *scientific information*. How is one to define scientific information operationally? Scientific information is semantic in nature, which means that it must be understood before any measurement can be attempted. Measures according to information theory, by being applicable only to syntactic information, do not relate directly to scientific value. The output of scientific work, however, is the input of subsequent stages of knowledge production, which means that it can assume pragmatic value after being understood semantically. The pragmatic value of scientific information depends on the productivity it enhances in subsequent stages when used as a means of production. Who, however, is competent to understand scientific information? Only those who themselves are working in the field. But then the question is: how do those working in their respective field express the value they attribute to the theories, theorems, hypotheses and scientific facts they understand? The measuring rod of economic value is the preparedness of those interested in a particular item to pay for it. Yet, the output of scientific production is generally not sold for money, but published and thus delivered free of charge.

If the assessment of efficiency should turn out to be impossible without a comparison of inputs and outputs in terms of price, measurement of the economic performance of knowledge production is bound to fail. In this case, the question addressing the collective rationality of science would remain unanswered.

In order to get an answer, we have to ask whether citation is free of cost. Even though scientific information is published and thus delivered free of charge, it must not be used as a means of production without acquiring a licence to do so. The licence is acquired by crediting the source of the information in a citation. This leaves the question unanswered of whether the licence is free of cost.

Acquiring a licence to use pre-processed information as a means of scientific production would be free of cost if the only motive for doing science were the pursuit of truth. Why bother who else makes use of my findings if it is only the collective progress of knowledge that matters? Things change, however, if we account for the fact that a piece of information assumes scientific value only if it finds the attention of fellow scientists. Only the findings recognized in the scientific community count as scientific feats. Even the greatest discovery remains irrelevant if it does not attract the attention of other researchers working in the field.

Attention, accordingly, plays a two-fold role in scientific production. It features, firstly, as a *scarce resource*, as the energy economized on by thought economy. Attention features, secondly, as an *income* remunerating successful research. The income of expert attention lies at the foundations of the reputation you enjoy as a scientist. It would be hard to find a scientist with no care for her or his reputation. Accordingly, income of attention is as important an incentive for doing science as are the epistemic motives.

In terms of attention, citation is not free of cost. It means, rather, that the citing author transfers a part of the attention earned by their work to the cited author. Citation thus tests the preparedness to pay on the part of those scientists looking for pre-processed information as a means of production. The citation, moreover, tests the preparedness to pay on the part of those supposed to be competent enough to understand and thus to judge the value of the information in question. The citations a theory or a theorem draw on count how often they are used as a means of production, thus measuring their productivity. The citation process thus proves its usefulness as a measuring process of the pragmatic value of scientific information.

Even though it seems at first sight impossible to measure scientific information, we discover that there is an effective measurement of scientific output. Moreover, we face a regular market performing these duties with aplomb. The historical introduction of an open scientific literature can be seen as the emergence of a producer's market for scientific information. Scientists offer their own product as a means of production for subsequent stages of knowledge production. The product is sold not before its re-use is documented by way of citation.

For any given piece of information, being cited functions as a proof of productivity. For the author, being cited means the earning of attention. It is only through being amply cited that you can grow rich in terms of expert attention. On the other hand, there is nothing you can do better for the collective advancement of science than being productive in the eyes of those competent to judge the value of cognitive work. Citations can thus be looked at as a viable, though imperfect, substitute for truth (which is non-operational in science since theories, by being doomed to be provisional, are unable to be definitely true).

But does that mean that scientists are doing exactly what they are supposed to do when maximizing citations in the way entrepreneurs maximize profits? The question is delicate. It concerns the principal role that non-epistemic motives play in leading collaborative knowledge production to efficiency.[4] Efficiency in collaborative knowledge production means that the resources at its disposal are allocated in a way that maximizes the collective progress of knowledge. Progress of knowledge

[4]The discussion of the role that non-epistemic motives play in collaborative knowledge production goes back to Philip Kitcher (1993, Chap. 8). Kitcher asks whether a philosopher-monarch interested in organizing the scientific workforce so as to promote the collective achievement of significant truth should give his blessing to the mixing of epistemic and non-epistemic motives (p. 305). Kitcher pursues his argument by reconstructing the strategies that rational researchers will apply when confronted with information challenging established theories. He considers two kinds of researchers: epistemically pure ones, and those whom he calls scientific entrepreneurs. The purists are motivated by intrinsic intellectual rewards only. When confronted with heterodox theories, their only concern is to reach an epistemically valuable state. For entrepreneurs, both epistemic value and personal success are important. Moreover, entrepreneurs are successful only if credited with success, where credit is a function of perception by others. Entrepreneurs must both compete for priority and sell their product. By comparing the collective outcome of the strategies applied by purists and entrepreneurs, Kitcher is able to show that a population of entrepreneurs is far from being doomed to perform epistemically worse than a population of purists. In contrast, the entrepreneurs promise to fare better than the purists for reasons of cognitive diversity and division of cognitive labour. Kitcher does not investigate the conditions under which scientific entrepreneurs will judge the information produced by others carefully and express their judgment honestly. His approach is inspired by game theory and population biology (p. 305). He treats science as a process in which cognitively limited biological entities combine their efforts in a social context. This context is not specified as an industry, however, where scarce inputs are transformed into cognitive output. Nor does Kitcher consider the circumstances under which success is credited in science. His consideration of non-epistemic motives, accordingly, does not go as far as asking whether scientists are doing what they are supposed to do when maximizing citations in the way entrepreneurs maximize profits.

cannot be measured from outside, but assessed only from within by querying the preparedness to pay of those looking for pre-processed information for their own production. For the working scientist, this indeed means that her or his contribution to the collective progress of science is optimized when the attention received from their fellow scientists is maximized. This conclusion is the first step to assessing the potential hidden in the functioning of scientific communication as a vanity fair. The next step involves the question of whether maximization of citations as the ruling motive of the working scientist is sufficient for securing efficiency in collaborative knowledge production.

The Limited Gauging Performance of the Citation Count

Scientific communication is not just an exchange of information, but a market where information is exchanged for expert attention. The question of whether scientists are doing exactly what they are supposed to do when maximizing citations in the way entrepreneurs maximize profits concerns the performance of the market in gauging the value of the items exchanged. The performance of markets crucially depends on two conditions: first, on the social control that competition amounts to; second on the incentives set by the earning potential. Citations are valid as a measure of pragmatic information only if earned honestly and accounted properly. Plagiarizing, faking data, arranging citation cartels, or playing off power relations in the editing and reviewing process are not unheard of in scientific communication. Notoriety of these kinds of misconduct testify to the virulence of non-epistemic motives in the citation process. From a purely epistemic point of view they are plainly nonsensical. Running scientific communication as a competition for attention thus proves to involve risks which cannot be avoided unless hedged by means of social control.

In scientific communication, there is no agency responsible for social control. Those competing for attention have to control one another. In order to dispense with personal surveillance, misconduct has to be made risky for the would-be wrongdoers. In a vanity fair, uprightness will reliably prevail only when the risk involved in playing foul outweighs the rewards of prestige that those in the competition are seeking. In science, misconduct is risky indeed. The risk of being exposed depends on the effectiveness of social control. Social control in markets, in turn, is a question of competition. Competition, though never perfect, strongly differs in effectiveness. Effectiveness depends on the number of competitors and, in particular, on the gain that is at stake. The higher the prospective gain of attention that the competition is fought over, the more effective it tends to become. The good news, therefore, is that social control in the competition for attention intensifies by the same factor as the temptations to foul play grow. It may be easy to pull the wool over the eyes of editors, referees and the readership of an institute's publication series that primarily serves the interest of its faculty in filling publication lists, but it is not so easy (though it does happen nonetheless) to succeed with empty pretension where the stakes include the candidature for a Nobel Prize. At these altitudes, competition may be deemed to approach—though never reach—perfection.

Yet the effectiveness of social control is not the only condition on which the evaluation performance of markets depends. The other concerns the translation of the earning potential into clearly circumscribed incentives to compete. The earning potential lies in the attention that researchers demanding pre-processed information are prepared to pay. The attention paid in terms of citations is no homogeneous quantity but one of differing quality. The quality varies with the recognition the payment transports and with the esteem the receiver has for the payer. A citation expressing respect or even admiration for the contribution credited is clearly worth much more than a critical or derogatory one. Equally, a citation from a highly competent and widely acknowledged colleague is different in weight than that of an unknown. These differences were tacitly accounted for as long as it was possible and reasonable to keep an overview of the entire publication process— which indeed scholars up to the 19th century were able to do. There is thus reason to assume that only a negligible amount was lost in the translation of the earning potential into the incentive of earning citations. The overview, however, was increasingly lost in the ever-rising flood of publications.

The output of scientific literature, be it measured in the number of scientific journals, number of publications or number of abstracts, has grown exponentially over the last two or three centuries. Depending on what one measures and how, the crude size of scientific information tends to double within a period of ten to fifteen years (de Solla Price 1963, p. 4f). Science is striking proof of Herbert Simon's thesis that a wealth of information creates a poverty of attention. Nobody is any longer able to keep the overview that once could be expected as standard. Knowledge production finds itself confronted with a novel kind of thought-economic problem. Unaided attention is overwhelmed by the sheer magnitude of the market for means of production. A new demand has arisen for means of enhancing efficiency in the search for pre-processed information. Attention, once more, finds itself asking for technical aids. The technological solutions to this need are online publication, search engines and *scientometrics*, i.e. methods of automated monitoring of the publication process and indexing of the citation process algorithmically. With citation indexing, technical support in navigating the flood thus extends to the introduction of an automated banking system for citations.

Technologies of such power are rarely limited to raising the efficiency they are supposed to improve, but often generate side-effects that tend to be overlooked by their early pioneers. With the automated accounting of citations, the problem of measuring the pragmatic value of scientific information seems to be solved algorithmically. In fact, the delicate gauging of scientific value is reduced to a mere counting of citations. Citations are added up as if the attention whose payment they document were measurable in homogeneous units. They are all tallied irrespective of whether they are approving or critical, detailed or superficial, thoroughly thought out or just meant to display up-to-dateness on the part of the citer.

The incentive to maximize citations thus no longer matches one to one with that to produce what is most useful in the eyes of those both capable of understanding and competent in judging a scientific work. The world of citations can also be gamed by exploiting the lack of overview and the widening habit of reading only keywords and abstracts. Where it is hopeless for critical scrutiny to cope with the flood of publications, strategies of marketing and competition for sheer visibility turn into viable options for determined citation maximizers. The option is all the more appealing since all those who are just looking for useful information have to cope with the overflow as well. If you are unable to keep the overview you have to resort to ways of browsing and guessing which, by their very nature, are prone to salesmanship. Visibility management has become a necessary basic skill in the scientific competition for attention, since performance is tracked by the citation indices in the way companies' business performance is tracked by stock quotes. Inadvertently, the focus thus shifts from rank in cognition to bibliometric ranking. The preoccupation with visibility is not without noticeable effect on the quality of supply. It is not uncommon to observe that work with rather a shallow draught proves remarkably apt at earning citations, whereas substantive work is omitted because published in print only or in a language other than English. Characteristically, the main supplier of indexing services is Google. Even though Google does not ensure that the information is complete or accurate, and Google Scholar is far from reliable, it has become the de facto standard of citation indexing. Moreover, it has become the standard access to scientific literature. Online accessibility of scientific literature, as convenient and labour-saving as it of course is, has subtly changed the vanity fair that scientific communication still—if not all the more—represents.

The wage of fame, once having turned the vice of vanity into the virtue of a well-founded incentive, runs the risk of failing precisely where it enjoyed its original success. Science gained enormous benefits from utilizing the pursuit of attention for corroborating the appeal of curiosity. Key to the translation of the earning potential into a well-founded incentive was the solution it found to the measurement of the pragmatic value of scientific information. Under the condition that the measurement works perfectly, scientists are indeed doing precisely what they are supposed to do if maximizing citations. Yet, perfection in measurement is incompatible with the counting of citations as homogeneous units. It is incompatible, thus, with the bank-like accounting that the now common calculation of impact factors relies on. Instead of rationalizing the measurement process, automated accounting promotes a sham accuracy which threatens to revert that turn of the vice of vanity into the virtue of a well-founded incentive. By reducing attention to a currency, it not only fails to measure what it is supposed to measure, but also obfuscates the phenomenal quality from which the motivational power of attention income ultimately stems.

The sobering view of scientific communication as a vanity fair sheds light on both its strengths and weaknesses. By providing evidence of a tendency towards efficiency in collaborative knowledge production it also lays bare what prevents overall efficiency. Its upshot, however, is that the pursuit of attention itself does not stay unscathed. What still must be taken into account, however, is the role played by upward bias in the valuation of the earned attention.

The Upward Bias in Scientific Communication

In contrast to the temptations of plagiarizing, faking data, building citation cartels, pretentious impression management and the like, the upward bias does not meet tightened control when the stakes grow high. In contrast, the higher the stakes in the competition for scientific renown, the higher the surge of the upward bias in the valuation of attention. No Nobel Prize was ever won without massive support from this bias. But despite its discriminating partiality, no referee ever vetoed its influence as foul play. The upgrading of the wealth of the wealthy rather works like the tax rebates granted to dominant companies by countries preoccupied with attracting foreign investors. In the case of attention, the subsidies are not so easily detected since they are granted not by a central agency, but emerge from the most common susceptibility of personal esteem to the esteem the person enjoys among third parties. Just as common as the inclination to discriminate according to income class is the reluctance to confess to it. It will be hard to find a scientist admitting to discriminating between attention-rich and attention-poor.

In scientific communication, accordingly, the bias is most easily identified where money comes into play. The money, characteristically, is not earned by the scientist but by the publisher. Scientific publication flourishes wherever enough money can be earned by publishers and enough attention can be earned by researchers. From the time these conditions were first met and established, scientific publication became a growth industry. This growth, in turn, fostered organizational development and refinement.[5] The journals, editions and conferences not only increased in number and degree of specialization, but also increasingly became ranked according to reputation. With ranking according to reputation, however, as inevitable and even helpful it may be for an initial discrimination between insignificant material and presumably valid work, the upward bias got a vital boost in scientific communication.

True, blind publication would have the disadvantage of a substantial waste of attention in looking for useful information. In order to accumulate and maintain reputation, agencies developed techniques such as the referee system. Nevertheless, ranked reputation, in the hand of the publisher, is key to the deployment of monopolistic power in the journal and book market. Organs of publication that leave behind their competitors in terms of reputation enjoy the capacity of setting prices on the market. Under conditions of perfect competition, market prices are determined by competition alone. No one person, whether seller or buyer, has the power to set prices. It is only when competition becomes monopolistic that prices can be set by suppliers (or monopsonic buyers). High-ranking publishers can—and indeed often do—set prices, thus exploiting libraries and readers relying on the supply of highly-ranked information. The financial misery of institutions having to supply researchers with scientific information as a means of production is a subject of constant complaint: they are bled by having to finance the surplus profits of publishers monopolizing top-ranked information.

[5] It shaped, moreover, the literary style of presenting scientific theories and facts. See Gross & Harmon (1999) for an account of the forces shaping the scientific paper as a literary genus.

But that is not all. The monopolistic distortions of the market for scientific information go further. Highly-ranked organs can also exploit their monopolistic power by marketing the wealth of attention their authors call their own. By granting high-impact effectiveness, they are of particular interest for well-known and prominent authors. In terms of reputation, such organs can provide out-and-out wealth management to prominent authors. If you are rich in attention, you are offered investment opportunities for your wealth that average scientists can only dream of. You will be offered placements in editions and conferences that grant superior visibility. You will be offered, in terms of wealth management, investment opportunities that grant attention revenues far beyond the average return from the publication of scientific information.

For scientists working for the wage of fame, the opportunity to be published in prestigious journals is hard to turn down. Being published in prestigious journals means getting a considerable head start in the run for citations. Having to maximize one's account of citations entails having to care about playing the maximization game in the highest possible league. This applies even in the absence of wealth management services. The reason is that the upward bias in the valuation of received attention is as pervasive in science as it is in the lifeworld in general. In science, however, we indeed encounter an empirical proof of the phenomenon.

Since the citation process is monitored and charted statistically, a remarkably uneven distribution of citations is observed. There are few who receive many citations and many who get just a few. The distribution curve is so clearly skewed that the phenomenon has captured the attention of sociologists of science since the inception of the discipline (Lotka 1926).[6] Merton (1968) called the conspicuously uneven distribution the 'Matthew effect in science'. The Matthew effect refers to the biblical parable of being entrusted with talents, the text reading: "For to every one who has will more be given, and he will have abundance; but from him who has not, even what he has will be taken away." (Matthew, 25: 29 RSV).

The skewed distribution of citations is not reducible to an uneven distribution of publications authors call their own. When counting publications instead of citations, the skewed distribution gives way to a normal (Gaussian) one with few extremes on both sides and the masses topping out around the average. An explanation for this phenomenon goes beyond mere productivity. The Matthew effect is due to our inclination to not only pay attention to one another, but also to take notice of to whom others pay attention. We consider it highly significant when observing that our fellows agree to give massive attention to particular persons. This raises our interest and our own preparedness to spend. Wealth of attention, to put it differently, works as an attractor in itself. If you are well-known, prominent or even famous, you are paid attention not only for your talents and merits but also for the very reason of being such a big earner of attention. Even though this tendency of wealth to augment itself may seem irrational, scientists are not immune to it. Scientists, just like vast swathes of society, pay homage to renown, prominence and fame. And they do so, as the Matthew effect in science discloses, even in terms of citations. They prefer to

[6]The pertinent names are Alfred Lotka, Derek de Solla Price and Robert Merton.

cite authors who are well-known, even if it means shunning those who may be more brilliant or innovative.

Economically, the explanation of the Matthew effect lies in the activation of wealth as an interest-bearing capital. Both form and function of this capital are different, however, from capital as a pre-produced means of production (as in the case of e.g. scientific information) that is paid for raising the productivity of the labour making use of it. Receiving attention for being rich in attention terms is an epitome of 'unearned' income. In economic terms, this kind of income is a rent. In the economy of attention, the class enjoying this rental income are those in the club of celebrities. Celebrities are the class of people who are not only known, but known for being well-known (Van Krieken 2019). And they are wealthier in attention than merit alone has earned: their extraordinary wealth accrues simply by virtue of their celebrity status.

The commotion around celebrities is hardly surprising in a community encouraged to work for the wage of fame. The rent accruing from wealth of attention may even be considered as a bonus that makes a scientific career especially attractive for the highly talented and ambitious. It is the wage of fame, in the purest sense of the term. The prospects of the bonus turn this wage into an extremely powerful incentive for those who believe they have a chance to obtain it. Science might be a good deal poorer in geniuses if the prospect of this superior reward were not available.

Yet, the appeal has dubious value. The social benefits connected with the prospect of fame have their counterpart in the social costs of rent-seeking and abysmal differences in income and wealth of attention. The accrual of rent, to begin with, interferes with the ability of attention income to serve as a measure for the earner's productivity. The attention prominent scientists receive bears no clear-cut relation to their productivity. In fact, it may come into conflict with the attention their current production deserves. The homage paid to prominence adds to the imprecision of the measurement that already suffers from the preoccupation with visibility and the looseness of social control. It endangers the self-organizing tendency toward efficiency from within.

The corrosion thus creeping in may seem of minor significance as long as Matthew effectiveness concerns only the happy few of the really rich. Matthew effectiveness, however, means increasing returns to scale. It concerns the gradient from the top all the way down. It infects the scientific economy of attention as a whole with traits of capitalism. Science, though lifted by the non-material nature of its economy from the lowlands of money-driven capitalism, might no longer be immune to the classical objections against capitalism. The capitalization of accumulated attention wealth even raises suspicions that class rule has entered the scientific economy. Must we face forms of exploitation and social conflict similar to those which pertain to money capitalism?

The answer could be affirmative if the reputation a person acquires through privileged access were inheritable. The answer would probably even still be affirmative if the class monopolizing institutional renown were also capable of monopolizing ownership of knowledge capital. Neither, however, is the case. Scholarly reputation, which essentially functions as personal property, cannot be transferred to other persons. Nor can authorship of scientific information legally be sold off. Accordingly, there is no inheritance of scholarly reputation, prominence and fame. Each scientist must start her or his career from scratch. Even the attention a person eventually receives for being renowned has the economic form of interest accruing from personal savings.

In science there are revolutions, but there is no class struggle. In scientific business, there are vested interests, but there is no propertied class monopolizing ownership of productive capital and personal wealth. There are forms of exploitation and social conflict, to be sure. These forms, however, are of a more harmless nature than the ones characteristic of money capitalism. Without playing down the blemish of the unequal distribution of opportunities, it is safe to state that the forms of reputation capitalism in science are superior to money capitalism in terms of distributive justice, as well as in terms of the allocation of scarce resources.

There is, however, a caveat, concerning the institutional framework within which the competition among persons is embedded. In money-driven capitalism, differences in personal wealth and income are overshadowed by the differences in power and influence exerted by firms. In reputation capitalism, differences in personal wealth and income are overshadowed by affiliation to research institutions. Science is not only the business of individual persons but also of organizations. As a rule, individuals participate in the market of scientific information as members of a university or research establishment. When competing for attention, they do so in their own name as well as in the name of the organization they represent. The organization participates in the income earned by its members. The share accruing to the research institute is accumulated and capitalized in turn. The capital thus generated is the renown enjoyed by the organization itself.[7]

It is here where forms of class rule enter the scientific business. The renown owned by the organization is an asset its members are free to exploit when competing with members of other research institutions. You are privileged from the outset when entering the competition as a member of a famous university or awe-inspiring research establishment. Conversely, you are handicapped from the outset if you are without recognized affiliation. However, whether or not you have access to such a privileged position depends not only on your talent and merit, but also on the place where you were born, and on the social class to which your family happens to belong.

The existence of a class ruling through institutional renown tends to impair distributive justice and efficient allocation at the same time. It leads to an allocation of talent and effort that is different from the one that would maximize the overall advancement of science. Whether or not this misallocation is deemed sufficient to undermine a presumed tendency towards efficiency, it yet discloses how far the influence of a bias that subtly emanates from the individual valuation of attention received may reach.

[7]The same applies at the level of nations. Manfred Bonitz and his collaborators have shown that the Matthew effect also operates with respect to countries. See Bonitz et al. (1997).

References

Bonitz, M., E. Bruckner, and A. Scharnhorst. 1997. Characteristics and Impact of the Matthew Effect for Countries. *Scientometrics* 40 (3): 407–422.

Descartes, Renée. 1637, 1968. *Discourse on Method and the Meditations*. Trans. E.F. Sutcliffe. London et al.: Penguin.

de Solla Price, Derek J. 1963. *Little Science, Big Science*. New York: Columbia University Press.

Franck, Georg. 1999. Scientific Communication: A Vanity Fair? *Science* 286 (5437): 53–55.

Franck, Georg. 2002. The Scientific Economy of Attention: A Novel Approach to the Collective Rationality of Science. *Scientometrics* 55 (1): 3–26.

Franck, Georg. 2015. The Wage of Fame: How Non-Epistemic Motives Have Enabled the Phenomenal Success of Modern Science. *Gerontology* 61(1):89–94.

Galison, Peter. 1996. Computer Simulation and the Trading Zone. In *The Disunity of Science: Boundaries, Contexts, and Power*, eds. Peter Galison, and David J. Stump. Stanford, CA: Stanford University Press.

Gross, Alan, and Joseph Harmon. 1999. What's Right About Scientific Writing? *The Scientist* 13 (December, 9, 1999):20–233.

Husserl, Edmund. 1935. *The Crisis of European Sciences and Transcendental Phenomenology: An Introduction to Phenomenological Philosophy*. Trans. David Carr. Evanston, Ill.: Northwestern University Press, 1970.

Kitcher, Philip. 1993. *The Advancement of Science: Science without Legend, Objectivity without Illusions*. New York: Oxford UP.

Lotka, Alfred J. 1926. The Frequency Distribution of Scientific Productivity. *Journal of the Washington Academy of Sciences* 16 (12): 317.

Mach, Ernst. 1883. *The Science of Mechanics*. Chicago: The Open Court Publishing Co., 1911.

Merton, Robert K. 1968. The Matthew Effect in Science. *Science* 159: 56–62.

Ravetz, Jerome R. 1971. *Scientific Knowledge and Its Social Problems*. Oxford: Clarendon Press (new edition: London: Transaction Publishers 1996).

Rescher, Nicholas. 1989. *Cognitive Economy: The Economic Dimension of the Theory of Knowledge*. Pittsburgh: Pittsburgh University Press.

Van Krieken, Robert. 2019. *Celebrity Society*. The Struggle for Attention. 2nd ed., New York: Routledge.

IV The Economy of Attention in the Age of Neoliberalism

The age of neoliberalism is an era of unleashed market forces, symptomized by the flourishing of vanity fairs. The unbound forces of capitalism are epitomized by what are now called the financial industries. The recent upsurge of vanity fairs takes shape in so-called celebrity culture. The question thus is: are we facing a merely accidental correlation between financial industries and celebrity culture, or is there a common causality waiting to be identified?

The answer is not entirely obvious. First, it is unclear whether there is a correspondence between the economy of attention and the neoliberal agenda in money-driven capitalism. Second, vanity fairs, in contrast to the attention economy at large, still wait to be taken seriously as economic phenomena. It is only in sociology where celebrity culture has given rise to a discipline dedicated to the phenomenon.[1] Economics, as pointed out above, has left the phenomenon aside to avoid methodological problems. In cultural criticism, celebrity culture has remained a predominantly polemical term. Third, the answer as to how celebrity culture relates to neoliberalism depends on how neoliberalism is distinguished from classical liberalism. In the jargon of its left-wing critics, neoliberalism is just radical—and thus ruthless—capitalism, fighting tooth and nail against any attempts by political rivals to tame it. What tends to be overlooked in the heat of the debate are its origins in economic theory.

The Neoliberal Agenda

Let us start with the latter point. Traditionally, economic theory deals with the working of markets. Markets are systems of decentralized negotiation and voting that connect the exchange of goods and services with the valuation (i.e. pricing) thereof. In theory, markets can be shown to be very capable, and indeed unbeatable information systems when it comes to the allocation of scarce resources according to needs

[1] For an authoritative overview see Robert van Krieken's recent (2019) standard work.

G. Franck, *Vanity Fairs*,
https://doi.org/10.1007/978-3-030-41532-7_5

and wants (as expressed by preparedness to pay). Classical liberalism translates this diagnosis into a political agenda. In principle, it gives decentralized negotiation precedence over central (i.e. state) planning but accepts the role of state intervention in the case of market failure. Neoliberals are less tolerant toward state intervention. They criticize classical liberals for assuming the state to play the role of a neutral, non-self-interested agent of social welfare. In fact, so runs the argument, politicians and bureaucrats are no less self-interested than businesspeople. According to the neoliberal doctrine, unbiased state intervention should not be seen as the panacea for market failure, especially in light of the systemic weakness of the state as a provider of potentially marketable services. Only in cases where market failure is shown to significantly outweigh state failure may state intervention be justified. Suspecting that the public underestimates the level of state mismanagement and corruption, neoliberals generally clamour for privatization of public goods and state-run services. Their battle cry is deregulation.

Markets presuppose the goods negotiated and exchanged to be private property. By connecting exchange with pricing, the working of markets turns the goods and services offered into commodities—items made up and priced for being sold. Privatization of public goods and state-run services thus includes the commodification thereof and the subjugation of the pertaining parts of the lifeworld under the reign of commerce. Since markets are much more flexible in responding to individual preferences than government bureaucracies, commodification is prone to expand far beyond the once state-run services as soon as areas such as healthcare and therapeutic services, care of the elderly, education, security, and cable and wireless communication are deregulated. Since competitive markets enforce cost-efficiency and sustain a constant search for niches on the part of the suppliers, neoliberalism should prove a powerful amplifier of the general trend towards the commercialization of the lifeworld.

Creatures of Deregulation: New Media and Financial Industries

This tendency, though, is much older than neoliberalism. A telling example is the history of today's popular culture. Popular culture, in the form that most massively influences today's lifeworld, is industrially manufactured entertainment. Entertainment, however, could not grow into an industry before media were available that were technologically capable of realizing the reproduction of the information supplied. It was media such as rotary printing, film and musical recording that transformed traditional folk art into what we now call popular culture. By being distributed as copies for sale, entertainment became a marketable consumer good and thus a commodity. The media, in turn, assumed the character of information markets, combining technical reproduction with marketed distribution. This transition was, on the one hand, enforced and, on the other hand, obstructed when broadcasting became an option for distribution. Broadcasting is a much more efficient kind of distribution than the sale of data carriers, but it undermines the saleability of the information. By being broadcast, the information loses its commodity character and assumes, in its stead, the character of a public good. It is then freely available and consumable in a non-rival way. The consumption by an individual consumer does not detract from the amount available to others. Accordingly, radio programmes are featured as the paradigmatic case in Paul Samuelson's introduction of the concept of public goods to economics in 1954.

Broadcasting leaps the barrier of the sales counter, making the information freely and thus maximally accessible. By being turned into a public good, broadcast information suggests itself as a candidate for state-run provision. This suggestion was understood wherever broadcasting started as a public service. According to this understanding, state action is called for by a paradigmatic case of market failure. In order to turn broadcast information back into a marketable good, its most progressive property would have to be sacrificed: it would have to be encrypted to reprivatize it. Even though its consumption is non-rival, it would have to be turned back into an exclusive good. In the face of this alternative public broadcasting, even at the cost of a state-run monopoly, seemed to be justified. Not so for neoliberals, of course: for them the state, as an information monopolist, is a failure as such. The problem is just how to privatize the public good without destroying its most efficient distribution channel. The solution, for them, consisted in creating a business model that accounted for another peculiarity of information goods. In contrast to tangible consumer goods, the consumption of information costs not only money—but attention as well. Information is neither fixed nor ready-made, but rather the surprise value we extract from patterns. In order to create the surprise value, the patterns have to absorb live attention. Consuming information goods thus means to pay attention to what the pattern is supposed to represent. Marketing information, therefore, need not mean selling it. It can also simply involve the marketing of a medium that is capable of attracting the attention of the general public. This is indeed a golden goose in the context of the advertising industry. Hence, the business model for privatizing broadcast information lies in turning the provision of information from an end into a means. The public commodity of broadcast information is reprivatized by utilizing it as a means of producing attraction services for sale to the advertising industry.

The irony of the origin of scientific communication in those academies and learned societies as an entertainment business has a mirror image in media history. By leaving the selling of information for money behind, media entertainment finds itself adopting the market model of scientific communication: information is offered for attention in order to generate attention income. The entertainment business thus succeeds in translating the form of the producer's market of scientific communication back into the form of the consumer's market the latter once started from.

As it once looked odd in pre-modern science to forego selling the information one has produced laboriously for money, it seemed irrational in the entertainment business until not so long ago[2] to disseminate the information one has to offer for free. Since,

[2]There are precursors, however, dating back to as early as 1835. See Wu (2016, Chap. 1).

as a business model, it indeed seemed like a non-starter, free dissemination took some time to make its way through the business world. For the pioneers of neoliberalism, however, this oblique business model was a godsend. It looked to be a vehicle for popularizing the deregulation campaign. At the same time, it was to usher in a new era of the economy of attention. Media understood as information markets underwent a momentous change. It was the business model much more than the technological base that became the distinguishing feature of so-called new—as distinct from old—media. Old media are those still selling information for money (press, books, CDs, cinema etc.); new media are those bypassing the exchange of information for money in order to fully concentrate on the saleable service of attraction (commercial TV, most of the internet).

Capitalist traits were not altogether foreign in the way old media already dealt with attention. The press, cinema and the recording industry had developed into mass media by professionalizing the business and introducing technologies of mass attraction. Traditionally, strategies and techniques of attraction had been cultivated in crafts involved in fashion and furnishing. By virtue of the technical media, mass attraction became a matter of calculable costs and results. Vast sums of attention could be collected by cheaply disseminating technically reproduced patterns if only the right stimuli were coded. By thus collecting attention in novel orders of magnitude, wealth in attention could grow into novel orders of magnitude. A new class of the attention-rich appeared on the scene: the stars. With stardom, the Matthew effect had landed in popular culture—only to virtually explode. It was now that wealth of attention showed itself to be capable of being activated as an income-generating asset, and on an overwhelming scale. As a star, you get attention not only for your appearance and achievements but also simply for being such a big earner of attention. The wealth of attention a star enjoys is more than just conspicuous: it proves profitable. It has turned into financial capital—wealth multiplying itself according to its order of magnitude.

The reason for this wondrous property lies in the attractive force exerted by the display of prominent people. You can observe this attracting force at any social event or party where someone from the hallowed A-list appears. Suddenly, the person you are talking to is distracted by their presence and you find yourself listened to with only half an ear. If you did not know it already you are now shown the evidence that prominence means importance. Small wonder, then, that the prominence of a lecturer easily multiplies the audience of an otherwise identical lecture. Stars move the masses even if the performance to be expected is far from breathtaking. Or, to put it differently, you need celebrities in masses if you want to run attraction as a mass business.

With media such as TV and the internet, the technical hardware grows into an infrastructure that supplies information to every household just like water or electricity, simply to collect the attention spent by the receiver in realizing the information. The yield, moreover, is measured by way of audience ratings and page views, rendering the attraction of attention as a quantifiable commercial service. By thus measuring the attention channelled and redistributed by the media, attention itself undergoes a strange transformation. The attention exchanged interpersonally, the most individual gift there is, turns into a means of payment. By being measured in homogeneous units and made to circulate via anonymous exchange acts, it assumes the features of a currency. Just as one euro equals another, one percent of audience ratings or one page view equals any other. Attention thus turns into a quantity, measurable in homogeneous units.[3]

As a consequence of this homogenization, the economy of attention comes to exhibit a social product corresponding to the Gross National Product in money economy. Just as firms pursuing profit maximization as their ultimate goal, media are competing first of all for shares of the social product of attention. The greatest attention is attracted by the media that most accurately find out what the masses want to see, hear and read. However, the business of attraction does not stop at the publication of head-turning images, sensational headlines and catchy tunes. It must proceed to recruit and amass the crowd-pullers needed for the battle for attention. Nothing seems to be more suited to attracting mass attention than the display of wealth of attention. In order to run the large-scale business of attention, you have to enjoin those who are attention-rich to display their wealth. In order to be displayed, though, their fortunes in attention have first to be made. It is only through the media themselves that conspicuous wealth of attention can be built up. In fact, the media themselves act as credit banks, financing this build-up through granting attention income in advance.

The media invest presentation space and time in people whose appearance promises to raise ratings and page views. By measuring attention revenue, ratings and page views also facilitate evidence-based forecasts of future income generation. They thus also measure the expected attention that the medium can grant. The credit in attention is granted in form of the presentation space and time that the medium invests. The value of the presentation space and time invested depends on the medium's profilefp, i.e. on how much attention one can expect from an appearance in this medium's programme formats. The person who is invited to perform in the medium thus enjoys a credit of guaranteed attention. The credit taker is given an opportunity that would otherwise remain fantasy. If the investment works out, the medium finds itself entering a new branch of banking, and the credit taker is recommended for follow-up investments. Both partners, moreover, are envisioning a longer-term goal. They both know that there is a critical mass at which the wealth of attention starts to self-amplify. It is only when reaching this critical mass that you are selected as a candidate for being raised to celebrity. And it is only at this point that the economy of attention enters the phase of high finance. The power of media to elevate persons to the pantheon of celebrity relies on their ability to collect unprecedented amounts of attention by triggering a kind of chain reaction of investments in presentation time and space.

[3]See Franck (1989) for an early account.

Media celebrities[4] are the new class of super-rich who live on the social product of attention, as channelled and redistributed by the mass media. In the age of neoliberalism, celebrities are made by the media. It is only the media that have the means to collect the huge amount of attention which feeds the new class of the super-prominent. The media, of course, are not a charitable institution. They are the banks and stock exchanges in the economy of attention. The people whom they have elevated to celebrity status promise, through their own popularization, to enhance the medium's popularity. Investments into the building up of attractors are highly speculative and rather risky, to be sure. They are speculative in the sense that wild betting goes on, but also in the sense that the bet influences the business result. The higher the expectation that the public has of the attraction, the better prepared and targeted the placement will be. So the placement quotes a market value, which is in itself dependent on this quotation. The quotation can—like a self-fulfilling prophecy—harvest the income which is expressed by its expectation. Windfall gains may thus be enough to trigger a self-enhancing snowball effect.

This has an effect on the newly gained wealth. Media celebrities find their counterpart in the nouveau riche who made easy money on the stock exchange. You need neither be a child prodigy, a stunning beauty nor a brilliant performer in order to be carried up by the chain reaction of self-fulfilling prophecies. You just have to place the right bet, catch the right mood of the investors' market. The moment that catapulted the celebrity to instant fame and wealth will soon be forgotten, or at least superseded by other, new events. The star is a rising one, because (and as long as) everybody assumes that all other gazes are directed at her or him. The foundation for this wealth is far from the solid factual basis relied on by the prestige of old elites in the Bourdieu style. As a foundation, nothing more is needed than mass suggestion entertaining itself. Kim Kardashian, to name a case in point, is a celebrity indeed. But to which elitist standards should she comply? She will be a celebrity as long as the pertinent media will invest enough presentation time and space to keep her ranked in the quoted market values.

The similarity of media banking to investment banking is not accidental. The new media function both as banks and as stock exchanges in their own way. The amount of invested presentation time and space corresponds to a candidate's expected ability to attract attention. This strength is to a crucial extent dependent on prominence already gained; or, alternatively, the prominence pre-produced by manipulative presentation of the person. It can be said, therefore, that the presentation space and time invested

[4]The accent is on media since celebrity as such—the person's glitter of publicity—is no new phenomenon. It is an offspring rather of the differentiation of the private and public sphere characteristic of modern societies. Robert van Krieken, in his comprehensive sociological account of the phenomenon (van Krieken 2019), traces it back to the courtly world where the reflection of royal attention was worked into the ultimate form of decoration. The shine could be passed, i.e. further reflected, to those surrounding the receiver who, in turn, could it pass it to her or his own surroundings. The hierarchy thus emerging took an initial step towards the emancipation of celebrity from merit. It foreshadowed celebrity society in its preoccupation with gossip as a way of socializing, accompanied by a creeping replacement of conquerors, military heroes, statesmen and religious leaders as cultural totems with celebrities of whatever kind.

quote a market value of capitalized income in attention. Audience ratings and page views measure the business result. Comparing investment with a business result is the way capital shares are priced by the stock exchange. Because this pricing significantly influences the subsequent development of the share prices there is more at stake for the person presented than just the immediate gain in attention. The maintenance of the market value of the capital one calls one's own always remains of concern.

Material and Mental Second-Order Capitalism

By leaving behind the exchange of information for money, the new media perform a decoupling from the "real" base of the economy strikingly analogous to the one performed by finance in money economy when developing into what came to be called the *financial industries*. Financial industries do not sell credits to borrowers to be turned into real investment, but only package credits given to derivative capital that entitles subscription for profits. Trading with derivatives has proved much more profitable than the retail trade of loans. By the same token, the new media do not sell the information to the consumers demanding it, but package the attractive force of the information disseminated into the derivative form of a marketable service. Again, trading with the derivative has proved much more profitable than the retail trade of information. In both cases, we are dealing with a second-order kind of capitalism ushered in by deregulation.

Deregulation lies at the base of the transformation of classical finance into the neophyte financial industries. Traditionally, client-based deposit banking was clearly separated, both by written and unwritten law, from transaction-based investment banking. The business of deposit banking is the translation of deposits into credits. It is committed to the long-term interests of its clients. The business of investment banking used to be the trading of shares, conducted verbally, face-to-face, on the market floor of the stock exchange. Stockjobbers making the market in shares were separated from stockbrokers who carried out trades on behalf of clients but were not allowed to act as market makers themselves. This professional divide was abolished by Thatcherian politics of deregulation in the 1980s, allowing the whole industry to consist of broker-dealers. At the same time, the screaming crowds on the market floors were replaced with online communication between traders' floors spread across the globe.

Online trading on globalized capital markets is short-term and fast, exploiting price fluctuations through comprehensive overview, analytic power and speed. A keyword of online trading is arbitrage, the exploitation of price differentials between markets or between observed prices and prices estimated by data analysis. These price differentials tend to be small and short-lived, but can be exploited profitably with computers scanning a large number of prices and exercising trade automatically. Those arbitrageurs with the fastest computers, shortest reaction times and most expertise take advantage of series of small differences that it would not pay to react to if taken individually. Small price differentials amount to considerable sums when multiplied by huge transaction volumes. Accordingly, the financial industries are addicted to cheap money. They are the clientele best served by so-called quantitative easing, the low interest-rate policy of the central banks. Quantitative easing, designed to stimulate the retail business of granting loans to the real sector, proves to be much better suited to fuelling speculative investment banking, thus continuing deregulation by other means.

The exalted school of investment banking is the 'making of markets'. In order to make a market, you have to do something that is noted and reacted to by the scene. One of the best-proven strategies for doing this is to come up with a novel kind of product. In fact, a flood of new financial products in the 1980s announced the arrival of a new kind of capital market. The financial industries started by switching from selling credits to borrowers to only packaging sold credits to derivative capital, entitling subscription for profits. Even though this new business model looked odd to mature business people, it opened up opportunities that left the retail trade of loans far behind. The new markets opened unprecedented opportunities for market-making strategies. By packaging credits into derivatives, immediate assessment of the creditworthiness of the creditors and detailed oversight over the deposited securities became inscrutable to the average purchaser; such appraisal was thus instead turned over to rating agencies. Loosening the connection to the real economy opens a leeway for speculative betting, i.e. for a second order of making markets. For making markets in an environment highly susceptible to price fluctuations, you have to perform transactions that cause a stir by changing the financial landscape. When successful, the strategy triggers the snowball effect on that on which you bet. Most probably the initial move which caused the price movement will soon be forgotten, leaving the fluctuation alone as the factor to which the market will react.

It was a remarkable concurrence that both finance and media took the opportunity, made available by deregulation, for a revolutionary change in their respective business models. Instead of directly responding to the respective demands for credit or information, they introduced an intermediate trade with derivative services, thus establishing another stage of commerce. On capital markets, there is not only a constant demand for opportunities but also of services that support the handling of risks. In the media, there is a constant production of patterns that are supposed not only to attract the attention that turns them into information but also to produce saleable services. Since investment is unavoidably risky, there is also a constant demand on capital markets for services of risk-taking such as insurance and hedging. However, as soon as there is an intermediate market for credits, these services can also be packaged alongside other derivatives into so-called structured products—in effect a sort of more complex derivative. Risk is taken by way of arbitrage; it is important to consider that risk is no coin toss or shot in the dark, but a calculation based on probability, relative to the level of information, overview and reaction time. The higher the risk as assessed by the market, the higher the profit chances of the skilled and knowledgeable arbitrageur. In the media, the derivative service meets an external demand. The service is produced as a by-product of the provision of information to the population. By finding the attention needed to realize the information, the service of attraction is implicitly co-produced. The attention thus attracted can be foisted information that is not actually demanded but realized inadvertently. All that remains is to package the service of this attention into a marketable commodity. The peculiarity of the attention captured in this way is particularly suited to addressing subconscious wishes and longings. It is this kind of attention that advertising is so keen on.

The Real Bases of Second-Order Capitalisms

It was only by decoupling an intermediate level of commerce from the "real" base of the economy that those forms of second-order capitalism could take hold. This is not to say, however, that the real base of the economy does not matter. Quite the contrary is true both in the money-driven economy and in the economy of attention.

The real base of the stunning upturn of financial industries was a global trend of redistribution. Until the 1980s the growth characteristic of industrialized post-war economies was distributed roughly equally between capital and labour, i.e. between the shares of profits and wages in GDP. By globalizing the value chains, jobs were mobilized towards low-wage countries to the effect that the bargaining power of the labour side in the organized distribution battle was appreciably weakened. Since then, the capital side has been able to appropriate the growth dividend more or less exclusively. In constant dollar income the median U.S. household income in 2012 was the same as in 1989, whereas the Dow-Jones index grew from 3000 in 1989 to 15,000 in 2012.[5] Capital gains thus grew by a factor of five (the average wealth of the 400 Forbes billionaires even grew by a factor of seven).[6] Profits, in contrast to wages, tend to be re-invested rather than consumed. The flood of money thus seeking investment opportunities was further magnified by the flood of cheap money generated by the low-interest policy of the central banks. It was by absorbing this unleashed supply of money that the financial industries could grow so big in such a short time.

The real base of the stunning upturn of the advertisement-financed media lies in that on which the financial power of the advertising industry relies. The advertising and placement services are bought by the suppliers of the advertised goods for two reasons: first, to exploit the economies of scale characteristic of industrial mass production; second, to utilize the potential of consumption to impress other people. These reasons are rather heterogeneous but complement one another perfectly. Industrial production is mass production where unit costs decline with increasing numbers. Increasing numbers of sold items thus equates to a rise in the efficiency of production itself. Efficiency considerations also play a role on the part of the consumer: efficiency in consumption means making the best of one's budget. Consumption has both a private and a social aspect. Our physical well-being is private, whereas our social well-being depends on what others think of us. In consumption

[5] And had surpassed 27,000 by mid-2019.

[6] The figures are from Stockman 2013.

terms, efficiency includes the consideration of the role one wants to play in other people's consciousness.

The real base of the financial power of advertising thus lies in the production function, as well as in the demand function, of consumer goods. It is demand, in the last analysis, that steers production. The challenge, accordingly, lies in teaching people how to utilize consumption for the pursuit of self-esteem. They have to learn how simplistic it is to think primarily of bodily well-being and comfort, given that one can also consume in order to be held in higher esteem by others—and thus ultimately by oneself. The advertising lesson starts by pointing out that consumption discloses taste and lifestyle. If your taste is secure and your lifestyle feels poised, then there is not much to learn—except, perhaps, that your lifestyle is expensive and your taste provides a constant temptation to overdraw your budget. If your taste is insecure and your expression of lifestyle feels shaky, however, a complementary disclosure of what the consumption signifies is welcome. This disclosure is the big challenge that advertisement faces. It is a challenge both regarding the signification of social status and the need to persuade the general public of the message of advertising.

When learning how to utilize consumption for converting money income into attention income, you find yourself, once again, facing that upward bias in the valuation of received attention. Even if you personally manage to stay indifferent, you will have learnt that other people pay attention to the kudos, renown and reputation of those paying attention to you. Utilizing consumption for pampering the ego thus suggests social climbing in the expression of taste and lifestyle. On the part of the education programme, this means that advertising has to single out elements of erstwhile luxury consumption now suited to being socialized with the help of cost-reducing mass production. In order to succeed, however, the meaning of the singled-out elements has to be understood not only by the prospective buyer, but by the general public as well. The turning of consumer goods into effective means for enhancing personal attractiveness thus faces the demanding problem of mass education.

In the case that there are signs of success in this kind of mass education, they may lead us on the track to the origin of the financial power that advertising deploys. Even though it may seem obvious that the regular and in fact inescapable exposure to advertising has left its traces in social psychology, signs that count should be of a more tangible and more easily observable nature. In the case that normal consumption has been turned into a regular means for taking care of personal attractiveness, the commodity form as such has to contribute to—if not incorporate—the solution to the aforementioned problem of mass education. Commodities as such should thereby have assumed a meaning that is generally understood as coding social status and membership of noted milieux.

The commodity form that business acumen has come up with to solve the problem of mass education is the *brand*. The brand is that component of items one can buy that deals with the social significance of consumption; it does not add to the material texture or tangible quality of the product but attaches images and stories supposed to evoke associations. Branding is of minor significance for consumption in privacy. Its field of action is the potential of consumption to influence what others think of us.

Since the potential is realized not before the representative consumer has learnt how to make use of consumption to impress other people, and these people have learnt, in turn, what the images and stories have to tell, the public has to be mercilessly bombarded with representations of the brand. Everybody has to learn that everybody else is also aware of it. The power of a brand depends on its prominence. It has to be not only known, but generally *known to be known*.

The exploitation of branding as a marketing device, though widely regarded as a nuisance that litters media programmes and the physical environment with adverts, subtly does its work. And it has seductive side-effects for both the consumer and the supplier. Branding gently hides the unsightly aspects of functionalizing consumption for purposes of attraction. Brands are not only well suited to influence what others think of the consumer—they are good at hiding the consumer's intention to impress. They make it easy to pretend that you buy the most expensive goods for their intrinsic value, even though you actually purchase them just to make other people take notice. In this regard, you are not even compelled to be honest with yourself in your pursuit of attention. Even the nature of the price markup paid for the sales promotion is hidden by branding. It is hidden since brands have become the common commodity form of marketable consumer goods. With branding, sales promotion has turned into a regular input to production, thus hiding from the consumers the surplus they spend on promotion.

Brands are what advertising is all about today. One can even say that the names or logos of things, by being heavily advertised, unavoidably turn into brands. They are indicators of attractiveness, thereby messaging what it means to be seen with the item. Advertising, accordingly, is only marginally concerned with product information. Its main concern is the promotion of images and storytelling that contextualize the brand in the lifeworld as shown in the media. Hence the dual use of celebrities built up by the media as both attractors for the media's own programmes and as actors in the advertisers' imagery and storytelling.

Branding is the empirically discovered and professionally proven means of incorporating into a product the promise that attractiveness is something you can buy. What the buyers of branded goods thus find themselves paying for is the counsel of how to turn money into attention income. The actual preparedness to pay goes so far as financing a complex of attraction industries that encompasses both the advertising agencies themselves plus their own supply chains and the media (broadcasting corporations and internet firms). It is these media that produce, with their own ramified chains of supply industries, the attraction services. The industrial complex thus financed is decoupled on the one hand from the interpersonal exchange of attention, and has on the other hand increasingly infiltrated it. Or, to express it the other way around, the economy of self-esteem is the source of energy that advertising has learned to exploit on an industrial scale.

By having turned brands into the normal form of consumer goods, advertisement has turned the pursuit of attention from the once elitist demand for prestige and self-realization into the norm of consumerist demand. Consumption, far from serving just physical well-being, now primarily serves the needs of self-esteem. The attraction industries' complex has solved the problem of mass education with sweeping success. Today, schoolchildren already have clear-cut ideas of what brands signify. Conversely, non-branded goods are saleable only at bargain prices. Such a success makes it seem almost petty to ask whether the consumers, having financed the overall industrialization of the attention economy, have got what they demanded. Preparedness to pay and real demand can differ in retrospect when the individuals' expenditure leads to collective results in which the individuals no longer recognize their aims. Looked at this way, it is far from clear whether the consumers who first welcomed the offer to buy the promise of attractiveness for money would have endorsed the collective result of a thorough commercialization of the traditionally rather informal and interpersonal economy of attention. In all probability, the very idea of advancing the vanity fair as a dominant market form in technologically advanced economies would have set tongues wagging. It is still an idea rarely associated with neoliberalism. It is only by taking this idea seriously, however, that the cultural dimension of neoliberalism comes to light.

The Last Contingent of the Anti-commercialism Movement

Consumer markets are not just any old sector of a market economy. They are the end-markets that all the value chains are targeted to and thus derived from. The rise of the vanity fair to the dominant form of consumer market thus amounts to a generalization of the particular role that competitions for attention had been playing in the independent cultural sector, a generalization that hardly seemed conceivable until not so long ago. Even though such a generalization can mean both that culture takes over commerce and that commerce takes over culture, it subverts the traditional distinction of culture and commerce.

Culture and commerce, according to this understanding, encompass the roles that production and consumption play in social life. The divide between culture and commerce is constitutive for culture as the field where values escaping valuation by money are created. According to this understanding, culture and commerce both deal with goods and services offered to the general public, but differ in the personal motives and organizational goals thereby pursued. Commerce deals with things for reasons of economic gain, i.e. for ends external to the things themselves. Culture, in contrast, is supposed to deal with things for their own sake. The paradigmatic case is art. Even though art can be dealt with as merchandise, artistic practice is supposed to be autonomous, i.e. serving only self-selected purposes and rules.

It was due to this understanding of culture that in the course of industrialization the introduction of those technical media was experienced as a severe crisis by cultural criticism. With technical means of reproduction, artistic information became a merchandise free of auratic originality. Copies capable of being mass-reproduced no longer claimed to be produced for their own sake. Rather, it was noted with horror that the more popular genres of culture were on their way to becoming regular industries, thus subverting nothing less than the essential difference between culture and commerce.

The strategy of defence that the elite of cultural criticism called for was an increased commitment of high culture to a decidedly anti-populist avant-garde ethos, thus decreeing strict discrimination against whatever tendencies there were of tolerating non-artistic motives in cultural production. Anathema to this avant-garde ethos became the *cultural industry* (which assumes a particularly pejorative tone in German as 'Kulturindustrie', the keyword of the Frankfurt School style of cultural criticism). Cultural industry stands for culture manufactured for purposes of economic gain.

References

Franck, Georg. 1989, August. Die neue Währung: Aufmerksamkeit. Zum Einfluss der Hochtechnik auf Zeit und Geld (The New Currency: Attention. On the Influence High Technology on Time and Money). Merkur no. 486, 688–701.

Samuelson, Paul A. 1954, November. The Pure Theory of Public Expenditure. The Review of Economics and Statistics 36(4): 387–389.

Stockman, David. 2013. The Great Deformation, Public Affairs Symposium on 'Conversation with Zombies'. *Journal of Consciousness Studies* 2 (4): 312–372.

Wu, Tim. 2016. *The Attention Merchants. The Epic Scramble to Get Inside our Heads*. New York: Alfred A. Knopf.

van Krieken, Robert. 2019. *Celebrity Society*. The Struggle for Attention. 2nd ed., New York: Routledge

V Deconstruction and the Fusion of Culture and Commerce

Ironically, the damnation of non-artistic motives in cultural production was a little bit overzealous. It overlooked the role that vanity fairs play in the art business, including the selection process of paradigmatic quality. It is simply not true that art flourishes only in an atmosphere uncontaminated by non-artistic motives. A piece of art, in order to acquire artistic value, has to pass a test that goes further than that of artistic beauty or truth. The work has to be recognized in the field, which means it has to attract attention in the art-appreciating community.

The strategy of high-minded cultural criticism closely resembles that purist line in the theory of science that equates autonomy with the avoidance of contamination with non-epistemic motives. It is indisputable, to be sure, that science has to be immunized against vested commercial interests. Yet, it would be counterproductive to ban non-epistemic motives altogether. An efficient allocation of attention in cognitive work does not only depend on the individual researchers' dedication, but also on what projects it pays to commit to in terms of the attention one can expect to earn. Investing one's own attention in order to get the attention of other experts, though seeming to be a kind of commerce, motivates the individual scientists to care about what others in the community find useful. Working for expert attention or, to dramatize it, working for the wage of fame, is certainly a non-epistemic motive. It means that scientists are expected to maximize citations in the same way that businessmen maximize profits. And it certainly means that scientific research is not done exclusively for its own sake. The evaluation implied in the remuneration with expert attention, though far from perfect as a selection process of scientific value, is nevertheless indispensable for implementing the organizational goal of maximizing the collective advancement of knowledge. A non-differentiating damnation of non-epistemic motives from knowledge production would thus be overzealous—if not downright counterproductive.

The banishment of non-artistic motives from cultural production may thus be overzealous as well. It would disable, if performed consistently, the valuation process built into the so-called discourse of art. The selection process of classics is as far from being a mere exchange of arguments, as is scientific communication. In both cases, it is the attention paid to the information supplied that tips the scales. In both cases we

G. Franck, *Vanity Fairs*,
https://doi.org/10.1007/978-3-030-41532-7_6

are dealing with markets of the vanity fair type. The selection process even works with the unstable dynamics of out-of-equilibrium markets. It utilizes the self-reinforcing dynamics of fashion and the self-destructing dynamics of inflation. Artists dedicated exclusively to the subject matter without caring for their presence in the discourse of art risk being rated as amateurs. At the very least there is the expectation that the professional artist cares about being acknowledged by other artists. The non-differentiating banishment of non-artistic motives from cultural production thus fails to appreciate the constitutive role that the selection of classics plays for art both as a profession and a social system. Inadvertently, thus, the strategy of high-minded cultural criticism does a disservice to art.

From Avant-Garde to Deconstruction

The philosophically well-armed fight against the contamination of culture with cultural industries was preparing the way for the end of the modernist avant-garde, which soon after found itself overtaken by a nouvelle vague of criticism. Deconstruction appeared on the scene and conquered the discursive vein of the discourse of art by force. It proclaimed the end of modernity, including the certainties on which it was built. One of the first certainties declared obsolete was that of an essential difference between high and popular culture. With hindsight it even seems that the art scene had simply been waiting for this pronouncement. It was all too easy to argue that: (1) Unshakeable truths are traditionally addressed as essences. If there are no such things as unshakeable truths, nothing is capable of being essentially this or that (2) So-called high culture is indistinguishable from elitist culture that serves as a means for the upper class to create exclusivity, i.e. social distance.

To address the first point: In the late 1960s deconstruction, spearheaded by philosopher Jacques Derrida and philologist Paul DeMan, marked the latest development in language philosophy. Derrida, its most influential proponent, came up with a radical criticism of the then dominant structuralist school. Until then, structuralism had been the unquestioned doctrine of the French theory of culture. It consisted of an elaboration and generalization of Ferdinand de Saussure's redefinition of linguistics (Saussure 1916). Saussure elegantly resolved—or, rather, circumvented—the notorious question of the meaning of linguistic signs, i.e. of how language, as a system of signs, relates to the world outside language. He came up with the astonishing conjecture that the meaning of linguistic signs (words, sentences etc.) is determined not by the things signified, but by a system of binary oppositions within the realm of signs itself. Language, thus conceived, is a totality of interrelated signs the meanings of which determine one another: *'un système où tout se tient'*. The grammatical categories thus find themselves defined completely by their function within the system. The system holds as a closed, consistent whole. It is this self-established stability which deconstruction dared systematically to call into question, thus challenging the dominant paradigm at its very foundations. Deconstruction starts by strategically presenting evidence that the system of signs that gains meaning by opposition to other signs is not a pre-stabilized whole. The meaning of words in ordinary language evinces a characteristic leeway of interpretation. In order to increase the precision of meanings or to improve the consistency of the system of signification, additional signs have to be introduced and references re-established. By adding signs, however, it is only the system of signs that is observed to grow. The gap between the signs and the signified definitely does not disappear. The leeway of interpretation stubbornly resists final resolution. Rather, the system of differences becomes a system of infinitely postponed capture of the objects by their signs. This combination of difference and deferment is what Derrida coined the *différance* (Derrida 1967/1997).

Différance deconstructs the very idea that the definition of concepts, i.e. the description of the meaning of words or of a given linguistic expression, can ever reach the things in their essence. It insists that there is no way out of language. The harder we try to do justice to the things as they exist outside language, the more we find ourselves adding only text. We have to take note that there is no way out of language. The whole system of descriptions, theories and proofs remains shaky and ever-changing. There are no such things as essences, i.e. eternally stable truths or unchangeable ideas, as envisioned in the example of Platonic forms. Since knowledge, in both its forms as philosophy and science, relies on language, there is no bedrock on which to ground something of the nature of absolute truth. At the heart of the message of *différance* is that the very idea of definite knowledge and unshakeable truth is a subterfuge; or, to come back to interpretation, the subtext inferred by an imaginative reader is as legitimate as the supposedly literal reading of the text.

To address the second point: Deconstruction, at any rate, hit a nerve with the zeitgeist of the time. It answered to the general impression of a thorough destabilization of the world of culture. The old boundaries were in a process of dissolution. With such prevailing conditions it is welcome news that nothing speaks against yielding to this dissolution. Despite its pointed intellectualism and a literary style exploring the edges of intelligibility, deconstruction was hailed in cultural criticism as a doctrine of liberation. With special preference, the new spirit rushed to subvert the distinction between so-called high and popular culture. This subversion was in line with the denouncement of high culture by the then highly influential sociologist Pierre Bourdieu, namely that it was just elitist culture set up by the upper class to create exclusiveness. It was certainly not the intent of Bourdieu to tear down the shielding of culture against commerce. Inadvertently and *contre cœur*, however, the mindset of deconstruction complied with neoliberalism in its call for deregulation. Even though it is hard to separate the influence exerted by cultural criticism from that which is due to the economic change in the cultural business, the border between culture and commerce became remarkably blurred.

Motives of Production and Origins of Applause

The border was flooded from both sides: by artists adopting commercial strategies and by commerce adopting artistic practices. Since the advent of pop art, the language and imagery of commercial mass culture have been imported into art; in the wake of the upturn of financial industries, artists such as Jeff Koons and Damian Hirst imported the traders' 'making of markets' into art as artistic strategies. The major subject of Koons' art is his own celebrity: he manages it with the skill of the trained investment banker, as indeed he is. Hirst celebrated, coincidentally on the day of the Lehman collapse, an unprecedented auction success at Sotheby's as a *chef d'œuvre d'art.*[1] These imports, to be sure, cannot be said to represent contemporary art as such: the artistic field, since then, is much too multifarious and heterogeneous to be represented by individual artists or even circumscribed schools. For every position, a counter-position can be found. These imports are symptomatic, nevertheless. By belonging to the most prominent and highest-priced representatives of contemporary art and by being those who most specifically react to the context of neoliberalism, they will be test cases for future art history regarding the selection process of classics. It will be interesting to see how the selection will deal with these tendencies—and, in particular, how the process itself, in terms of its very organization, will adapt to the levelling of culture and commerce.

No less specific than the adoption of financial strategies in contemporary art is the rise of so-called creative industries. Creative industries are those industries which, while thoroughly conventional, also play a key role as a driver of the latest regional and urban developmental policies. Creative industries epitomize the takeover of artistic practices by commerce. They are what the former branch of decorative arts has grown into by being subsumed into the supply chains of advertising and entertainment. The designers, copywriters, composers, photographers, art directors etc., dedicated to what advertisers and media providers demand, are definitely not artists in the sense of art for art's sake. They make use, however, of a developed body of know-how that is in constant flux as is the technique a professional artist controls. Creative industries are that part of art-affiné creativity that the attractive industrial complex manages to skim off. These industries, remarkably, work for the same dualism of markets that artists and scientists traditionally have been working for individually. They work at once for the market where works and services are exchanged for money—and for the market where information is exchanged for attention. The attention, though, is earned not by the designer, but by the client she or he works for, thus depriving the creativity of its autonomy. The steady course of the commercialization of creativity, this once characteristic and inviolable feature of culture, has now led us across the Rubicon, definitively fusing culture and commerce once and for all.

What once was the worst nightmare of cultural criticism has become reality. The attraction-industrial complex including creative supply industries represents the perfect realization of the once-maligned *Kulturindustrie*. The mainstream of today's culture is advertisement-financed media content. Unbelievably, though, nobody bats an eyelid at what was once decried as dystopia having become reality. Instead of loudly deploring the fusion of high and low, contemporary criticism oscillates between

[1] The sale generated £111,576,800-10 times that of the previous record for an auction dedicated to a single artist: the £11.3 million raised when 88 works by Pablo Picasso were sold by Sotheby's in New York in 1993. (*The Telegraph*, 16.9.2008).

welcoming the democratizing effect of generally accessible mainstream culture and condemning the neoliberal-minded business models of the providers. This conviction, however, is far from the earlier damnation of non-artistic motives in cultural production. It is acknowledged, whether explicitly or implicitly, that the damnation of non-artistic motives in cultural production failed to recognize the role that the discourse of art plays as a market where information is exchanged for attention. It turned a blind eye to what indeed separates the professional artist from the worker in the attraction industry. The artist need not be indifferent to applause but has to care about the side that applauds.

The main reason why cultural criticism acquiesced so comprehensively to the triumph of the cultural industry is that the fusion of culture and commerce was not the end of autonomous art. Artists such as Koons and Hirst, though assimilating commercial strategies, did not intend to be hailed as captains of cultural industry—and indeed would probably feel a certain distaste for such a moniker. They took it as a matter of course that they were acknowledged as distinguished representatives of autonomous art. What is not so obvious and rarely thematized in criticism is what this reliance is based on. In the horror vision of *Kulturindustrie*, the fusion of culture and commerce seals the end of autonomous art. Even economically it is far from clear how autonomous art, as a social system, can survive the fusion of culture and commerce. If there is no such thing as an essential difference between commercially-dependent creativity and autonomous art, the difference dwindles down to that between goods markets and vanity fairs. What, hence, was it that saved art from a hostile takeover? Or, to express it more pointedly: why did the gradient between high and low, though denounced and accursed in the discourse, not vanish?

In order to see clearly, we have to pay attention once more to the ambiguity in the meaning of 'discourse'. Discourse means both the exchange of information for information (as, e.g., arguments for arguments) and the exchange of information for attention (as, e.g., artistic content for considered judgement). Though regularly coupled, these sides do not coincide. Debate, for example, can agree in denouncing high culture while attention continues to be paid to art that addresses an exclusively educated and experienced audience. The market process, that is, does not correspond precisely to the course of debate. It must have been due to such a deviation that deconstruction, even in its heyday, left the separation of distinguished high culture from populist mass culture virtually intact. This deviation, to be sure, has nothing to do with the difference between goods markets and vanity fairs. It relies on the discrimination, on the part of the artist working for the wage of fame, between aesthetically educated and anonymous, mass-attracted attention.

It wouldn't have been a particularly promising move to insist on the constitutive role of this discrimination in the debate of those days. Discrimination between cultures or social groups was banned and despised as such. It is interesting, thus, to see how deconstruction, where adopted as a guideline for artistic practice, made the discrimination between aesthetically educated and anonymous mass attracted attention instrumental. The paradigmatic case, predisposed for exemplification, is architecture.

The Functionalism of Conspicuity

Architecture is the perfect example of the way that deconstruction replaces the distinction of artistic and non-artistic motives by discriminating between origins of the attention it earns for two reasons: first, architecture, like no other discipline of art, was obsessed with deconstruction; second, architecture, by its very nature, never allowed a dichotomy between artistic and non-artistic motives to develop.

Deconstruction, though seeming to contradict the very idea of building, was the most durable and eventually emblematic phase of postmodern architecture. Its origin in language philosophy notwithstanding, deconstruction is deeply ingrained in the design practice of postmodern architecture. It marked the final defeat of the modernist doctrine of functionalism. This doctrine, foundational to modern architecture, defined functionality reductively in terms of usability, economy and physical comfort. It fought ornamental forms of expression and ostentatiously rejected the inclusion of advertisement in the functions that architecture may be dedicated to. With deconstruction, a redefinition of functionalism began to prevail. Deconstruction gave birth to a *functionalism of conspicuity*, a functionalism that included the functionalization of architecture as a medium that sends messages and supplies entertainment in order to attract attention. It did so, which is precisely the point, without dismissing architecture's claim to be a classical discipline of autonomous art.

Architecture, indeed, has ever been both a discipline of autonomous art and a representative of what nowadays is called creative industry. Though autonomous, it is not a free but an applied kind of art. Architects professionally produce a commercial service, paid according to fee schedule. It is only in post-production that their work enters the market side of the discourse. In architecture, accordingly, culture and commerce have never been separated. The explanation, however, of how it was possible that language philosophy could become such a source of inspiration for architecture, lies purely on the cultural side of this duality.

The founder and main theorist of deconstructivist architecture was Peter Eisenman, an architect and architectural theorist who was interested in linguistics throughout his career. Having previously developed a sensibility for the illusions of cohesion and solidity that the concept of functionality had promised, he became fascinated by Derrida's radicalism of destabilization. He started to identify, in the perspective of the *différance*, allegedly unshakeable truths of architecture such as, for example, that buildings and building elements must have a function, that a building should give the impression of stability, that architecture has an author and that the users have a right to comfort. He then proceeded to assail this 'metaphysics of architecture' as he called it, using architecture's own means. The effect was extraordinary. All the world was astonished when he published designs of buildings which seemed to mock all functional logic, which seemed to be the result of collapses, which demonstratively violated the principle of usability. And the effect continues to cause ripples to the present day. It helped deconstructivist architecture to an overwhelming success.

Eisenman's message would prove a hit. It captured something of the zeitgeist and gave it architectural expression. Eisenman's buildings, indeed even the plans for his buildings, became media events. Haus Immendorf, the Alteka Tower and the Max Reinhardt Building became icons without ever being built.[2] But some deconstructivist designs did make it beyond the drawing board. They found builders who were willing to invest in the venture. Moreover, deconstructivism shaped the image of architecture at the same time that new media had begun colonize the internet. This coincidence cannot be explained by the intentions of the architects. Nor is it reducible to some will of design. Architecture is not just any art. It is the art that determines the image of our built environment. It is notoriously costly and binds expensive resources for a long time. An architectural style is never accidental. It reveals something about the society that has chosen it. It provides information on the willingness of society to pay for the representation of their values and concerns.

Disregarding the upsurge of the economy of attention, the very idea of an architecture of deconstruction would be plainly irrational. Eisenman, nevertheless, was concerned with the cultural significance of architecture. He observed that architecture was a strong medium as long as it possessed the power to inscribe into space differences such as profane and sacred, accessible and forbidden. This strength faded with the increasing weight of calculated utility and economic efficiency. The reign of commerce degraded architecture to a weak medium, at least in comparison to today's strong media, of which Eisenman (1995) names journalism, TV and advertising as examples. Strong, according to Eisenman, are the media that are dominant in the attraction of attention. In order to preserve the cultural significance of architecture, Eisenman prescribes strong medicine. Architecture has to take advantage of advanced strategies of disquiet and astonishment, as exemplified by cinema and computerized gaming. It is only through an extreme defamiliarization that he sees architecture being capable of closing the gap to the kind of pictoriality and novelty that today's strong media have developed for surviving in the unleashed battle for attention.

Thanks to its exposed intellectualism, deconstructivism was immune to populist temptations from the outset. It thus found itself aligning conclusively with the new defence line of autonomous art against the cultural industry. Instead of demonstratively refusing any kind of commerce, it merely snubbed applause from the wrong side. What counts is not the general public's preparedness to pay as measured by audience ratings, but expert attention, i.e. attention that is architecturally educated and intellectually responsible. What matters is the response from other architects and other theorists of architecture. The attention to be maximized is from those who themselves feature in the discourse of architecture. The measure of success lies in the internal hierarchy of the architects. It was in this ranking where Eisenman for

---

[2]For pictures see:

- Alteka Office Building, Tokyo 1991: https://www.moma.org/collection/works/1030.
- Max Reinhardt Building, Berlin, 1992: https://eisenmanarchitects.com/The-Max-Reinhardt-Haus-1992.

example was at the pinnacle in his time. He had demonstrated how to practice the functionalism of conspicuity without descending to the lowlands of populism. He even showed how one can, by demonstratively rejecting acclaim from the wrong side, enjoy a quasi-popular success on the right side.

However, in order to catch up with those strong media the quasi-popular success enjoyed in august quarters has to grow into an outright popular success without losing its speciality. The discourse, to put it differently, has to expand beyond the specialized literature, thus to earn attention also as measured in terms of audience ratings and page views. This requirement may seem paradoxical, but the school of deconstruction accepted the challenge by inventing the 'star architect'. The star architect is the ingredient needed for personalizing iconic architecture. Without a personality attached to it, a building, let alone a design, has hardly got what it takes to become a media star. The architect himself, however, is of course capable of being a celebrity—and thereby of imbuing his work with his star quality.

The star architect, though, is not just prominent, profiteering from their wealth exclusively. They are a provider of highly demanded services of design, and furthermore support the builder in publicity and negotiations with financiers and authorities. These services, though imbricated with advertising, are demanded of the architect as architect. Celebrity void of professional reputation does not qualify. Nor can a star architect's career sidestep the discourse of art.

The breakthrough of deconstruction in architecture was connected with a proliferation of star architects, reminiscent of the proliferation of star actors in the wake of the birth of cinema. Constitutive of the star architect are their design capabilities and telegenic appeal, as well as fluency of communication in post-structuralist jargon. The gesture of demonstratively refuting the applause of the masses on which a star nevertheless depends is a tightrope act indeed.

The Alienating Reduction of Attention to a Measurable Quantity

When looked at from the viewpoint of social economy, the star architect demonstrates how the cultural superstructure can successfully adapt to a changing economic base. When looked at from the viewpoint of art, the adaptation shows itself to be costly. The service as demanded by builders interferes with the dedication to the work in that laboratory where latent desires of taste are researched. Casting architecture into a medium supposed to catch up with those strong media in supplying entertainment for earning attention unavoidably affects the nature of the attention it deals with. Key to the alignment is the measurement of the service of attraction. Measurement of the service of attraction cannot help but deal with attention as a quantity, homogeneous and bereft of individuality, as is a currency. This reduction gives way to a fascination with the figures and rankings of wealth, and eclipses all those properties from which the value of attention income and the interest of the arts in exploring the human condition stem. What is so captivating about receiving benevolent attention is the feeling of being welcome, as an embodied consciousness, in another consciousness of one's own kind. What the arts are exploring when sniffing out desires that cannot be recognized but by fulfilment is the capacity of conscious experience. The arts explore, in ever new ways, how it feels to be human.

This 'how it feels' quality, to underline it, is key to both aesthetic perception and touching inter-subjectivity. In both ordinary and aesthetic perception, a feeling of being the perceiver is involved. In the perception that just informs the organism about its environment, however, the feeling of being the perceiver rests meekly in the background, contributing to the experience merely the impression of a kind of ownership. Merely informative perception turns into aesthetic perception as soon as the feeling of being the perceiver is affected in such a way that it gets into resonance with the percept. Aesthetic perception, to put it most simply, includes a feeling of being touched.[3] Disregard it and you have overlooked both artistic understanding and the delight of feeling welcome in another consciousness. The delight, however, does not disappear without leaving an afterimage. It finds itself replaced by a fetish for figures and rankings supposed to measure the wealth of attention.

This fetishism, small wonder, is cult in celebrity culture. Architecture has to join the cult if it is to become a strong medium such as TV or online media. In order to catch up, architecture has to learn to deal with Matthew effectiveness without disavowing its status of autonomous art. Matthew effectiveness relies on the fascination with figures and rankings that rate fortunes of attention like share prices rate the market value of firms. For securing the status of autonomous art, deconstruction resorts to the selection of an art-affiné audience by exposed intellectualism.

Architectural deconstruction thus affords a two-fold reduction: the reduction of attention to a measurable quantity and the reduction of art appreciation to intellectual proficiency. It is remarkable how long this extravagance found allegiance in the discourse. The alleged innovation of the employment of Matthew effectiveness and of selecting an art-affiné audience relies on forgetting that both have long since been firmly included in the discourse of art. As soon as the long-term and post-production selectivity of the discourse is accounted for, the career schema of classics shows itself to be a constitutive part of the discourse. The schema prescribes those phases of fashion and inflation. When looked at in this context, a design strategy that focuses on the Matthew effect from the very beginning is nothing more innovative than the attempt to jump the initial steps of the career schema. The strategy amounts to turning the triggering of the fashion phase into the very purpose of the design. Taken as a design strategy, it means to include, via anticipation, the post-production selectivity of the discourse into the design process right from the beginning. In the post-production career scheme, though, becoming fashionable is no end in itself, but a stage of social test, supposed to prepare the way for inflation. The Matthew effect, thus contextualized, carries an expiration date. Fashion inevitably ends in inflation, which is productive in the selection process of classics but deadly for managed conspicuity. Just how short-winded the strategy of anticipating the post-production

[3]The epitome of aesthetic perception is eroticism. Eroticism is the aesthetic surplus over sex.

selectivity of the discourse is, comes to light when the selection is extended to that of the art-affiné audience. Managed conspicuity has to resort to the selection of an art-affiné audience by exposed intellectualism. The selection process of classics turns out to be working, additionally and parenthetically, as the selection of candidates qualified for a leadership role in the discourse. The crucial and ultimately decisive step in the career schema is the resurrection out of the acid bath of inflation. For this resurrection, people competent in recognizing timeless artistic quality beyond novelty and rarity are required. It is here, to repeat, where the saying that 'it takes one to know one' applies: only those who themselves are either artists or of an artistic vein are equipped to recognize conclusively the rank of an artist démodé.

When classics are born, the canon is updated and obstetricians receive their qualifications, as it were. It is here where the core competence comes to the fore around which the discourse, if indeed autonomous and self-organizing, condenses. This process demonstrates how the self-selection of the art-appreciating audience extends to the recruitment of figures qualified as its speakers. This two-fold selectivity should certainly not be omitted when trying to explain both the incredible performance of the selection of classics and the continuing relevance of centres of competence in the art-affiné community. The core competence in both respects certainly includes intellectual skills for presenting and defending the discovery of the thus far latent desires of conscious life. The discovery itself, however, concerns the 'how it feels' quality of aesthetic perception. The core competence in artistic judgement thus forbids compliance with any reductive view of attention which could abstract this core of subjectivity away.

But how might it be explained, then, that the discourse so willingly gave way to this alienating viewpoint? There is a general and a specific answer. The general answer is that zeitgeist had—at least in theory—turned a blind eye to the subjectivity of attention it nevertheless is dedicated almost excessively to in everyday praxis. The specific answer relates to the basic impulse of deconstruction. A theory whose constitutive impulse is the subversion of firmly believed certainties cannot be expected to develop an in-depth understanding for the canon. The preoccupation with overtaking modernist avant-gardism leaves little room for taking into account the long-term, post-production selectivity of the discourse. What obscures the theory's view of the canon, in particular, is that the impulse of deconstruction is bound to miss it. Canonical quality is not something to be deducted from allegedly unshakeable truth—but rather found out by way of social proof. It is immune to deconstruction since it has nothing to do with pre-given criteria or essential properties; it relies on ongoing empirical test. Its method of determination consists of the two-stage test of first accumulating and then resolving fortunes of attention. Its modus operandi is a dynamic that turns self-amplification by its own momentum into self-destruction. This dynamic is immune to deconstruction since its rule is purely empirical and thus in power as long as it agrees with observation.

In the meantime, deconstruction has itself entered the long-term, post-production test of durability: it has landed in the acid bath. It now testifies that any employment of the Matthew effect comes with an expiration date attached. No-one knows whether the selection process of classics will detect someday, in the architecture of Eisenman and his school, significant contributions to the discovery of desires that have until now escaped identification. If, however, such a discovery leads to resurrection, it will have discovered properties of attention that fall victim to the minting thereof as a coin.

So far, the selection of classics has worked impeccably as the arts' inbuilt review process of self-correction. It is due to this 'context of justification' that art can afford an adventurous 'context of discovery' (both in Popperian parlance, see Popper 1934/1959), without having to insure itself against an oft-anticipated decline. So far, the post-production, long-term selection has worked reliably as a safeguard of autonomous art against its decay to something less erudite, ambitious and dedicated than the great laboratory. No work or even tendency of art has managed to climb the ladder up to the top without being recognized for some significant discovery in the field of sensuous intelligence. As long as the selection of paradigmatic quality and the recruitment of the pertaining sensibility are one, there is no reason to be horrified about experimental attempts within the art business world to raze tradition to the ground, as did modernist functionalism and resolute deconstruction alike. The experiments, in the case that their results pass the test of sensuous intelligence, will safely be incorporated into the achievements of the great laboratory. If they don't pass, they will dissolve at the latest in the acid bath. As proof of this, the most recent classics of architecture, taking Loos and Mies as an example, succeeded in finding ways of putting the sense of self of the perceiver into resonance with the percept, in spite of the claim that their architecture was purely functional.[4] While the question of whether there will be classics among self-confessed deconstructionists is yet to be answered, we may be confident that the vanity fair, having performed the selection since time immemorial, will continue to work with the accustomed scrutiny and reliability.

Vanity's Inherent Contribution to Commercialization

Might we infer from this capability of vanity fairs to do justice to the phenomenal nature of consciousness that the tendency to treat attention as a currency is actually foreign to self-organized competitions for attention? That the tendencies to alienation are due to rules of commercialization that are imposed from without upon the working of vanity fairs? For businessmen who deal with attraction services for monetary gain, the habit of treating attention as a measurable quantity is an almost inevitable *déformation professionnelle*. The same applies, *a fortiori*, to content providers who utilize prominence for purposes of attraction. This habit, however, obscures the view of the great laboratory dubbed art as well as the source of the power to which the attraction industry owes its shattering success.

For a pictorial illustration of the global megastructure of industries, infrastructures and information markets, the attraction industrial complex may be metaphorized as a

[4]Loos even refused to call architecture an art. See Loos (2009).

cathedral, erected for the cult of attractiveness and built of supply chains heading to the production of attraction services. The erection of the complex is financed by the advertising industry for the sole purpose of translating the dream of attractiveness, dreamt by so many, into the habitual preparedness to pay premium prices. The dream of attractiveness emanates from the psychic household that converts attention income into the asset of self-worth. Surveying this source, the image of the cathedral gives way to that of a hurricane emerging from an initial fluctuation by way of ever-expanding self-amplification. Apprehending the storm as it sweeps the lifeworld is therefore contingent on tracing the force of self-organization down to its origin in the individuals' pursuit of self-esteem.

Understanding the genesis and the level of development of the attractive industrial complex thus requires us to venture into the eye of the storm. In its midst we face the source of energy that drives the self-organization with ever growing efficiency and effectiveness: starting with the most casual emergence of vanity fairs wherever people compete in public with others in the pursuit of attention, proceeding to the use that society makes of such competitions explicitly for performing extraordinarily demanding tasks in the arts' and the sciences' contexts of justification, and then on to the build-up of the suction that sweeps society in its entirety and has culminated in the breakthrough of mental capitalism.

At the very centre of this storm we face the epitome of a feeling of being oneself: self-esteem. This peering down into the eye of the whirlwind thus amounts to nothing less than a thorough reflexion of affective self-consciousness. It requires a clear understanding of the dependency of this self-centred feeling on outer recognition, and of its way of converting outer recognition into self-realization. This conversion accounts for and, in a way, measures the attention earned. Still, it does not measure quantity only, but also accounts for quality. It takes into consideration the individuality both of the emotional charge of the attention received, and of the appreciation that the receiver has for the payer. The conversion thus accounts quite naturally, not to say instinctively, for that phenomenal quality of attention which falls victim to its reduction to quantity.

The Constitutional Frailty of Mental Capitalism

The reflexion, however, must go further. It must include the interface between the internal household and the social economy of attention. It is only by thus widening the perspective that the core question of how to react to the criticism of commercialization can be addressed. Vanity itself is no innocent motive. From the beginning it is unclear to what extent either the internal motive of vanity or the external rule of the market is responsible for the effects of commercialization in attention economy. It might be premature, therefore, to assume, as social criticism routinely does, that pre-established social and, in particular, power relations are responsible for the incriminated phenomena.

It is true, of course, that commercialization brings rules to bear that are external to the psychic household. The struggle of self-esteem, energizing the cult of attractiveness since time immemorial, has undergone a transformation that has cast relevant fields of the competition into the form of regular markets. This transformation, however, was no imposition of a pre-established market form, but the result of a process of gradually increasing effectiveness and efficiency in the business of attraction. Mental capitalism, accordingly, did not start with the subjugation of a dispossessed labour force under new conditions of production, but with a subtle re-education of consumers. Exploitation tacked a course from coercion to seduction. Even disregarding the money that is plucked from the pockets of consumers, there is exploitation in mental capitalism—witness the new class of attention super-rich. Celebrities are built up and deployed for skimming off attention from an audience who themselves have to care about attention income. Those in the audience give live attention and get cheap imitation pearls in return. Doesn't that mean that a propertied class exploits the people? In a sense, of course, it does. This exploitation, though, looks pretty strange. It carries features of collusion.

The exchange of emotionally-charged attention for mass-manufactured, anonymously disseminated information indeed relies on a kind of class rule. Class rule, however, is not the same as unbalanced exchange. Class rule is conditional on the imposition of the tribute. Yet, in the exchange of manufactured information for live attention nothing is imposed. Information suppliers, by responding with ruthless mass attraction to the consumers' preferences for celebrity, are certainly promoting class distinctions. But they can hardly be accused of exploiting the plight and helplessness on the part of the victims. The exchange, rather, is consensual. With regard to the ethical dimension, it may even be argued that the charge of ethical misconduct is on the part of those celebrating the celebrities. The preparedness to pay homage goes back to that discrimination in personal appreciation which we all employ according to our social status. The strength of the argument, of course, depends on how the iridescent character of exploitation unfolds in the further development of mental capitalism.

What we thus face are almost contradictory traits crossing in the attention-driven aspect of capitalism. The mental character of mental capitalism relies heavily on the upward bias in the valuation of attention. Remarkably, the upward bias, as utilized in the attraction business, shows both elitist and democratic traits. It is elitist in celebrating those at the top of the social hierarchy; it is democratic in being a norm established through a tacit majority vote. This tension, not to say antagonism, cannot be without repercussion on the condition and sensibilities of celebrity culture. It promises, in particular, to resonate with that general pattern of modernization in social change, already mentioned here several times. The pattern is that of the socialization of former luxury goods.

Paradigmatic cases of the socialization of former luxury goods include the elite villa with park transposed into the popular home with garden, the chariot into the mass-produced automobile, fashion moving from courts and salons to the high street—to name but a few. Egalitarianism hasn't vanished from the social agenda—it has merely changed its character. Instead of flattening the social gradient, status symbols are designed to trickle down into mass consumption. It is in line with that pattern of social change that, in the meantime, the latest addition to luxuriousness—celebrity culture—is itself subject to socialization. The key term is social media.

References

Derrida, Jacques. 1967/1997. *Of Grammatology, Original in French: De la Grammatologie*. Paris: Les Éditions de Minuit, 1967; Translated into English by Gayatri Chakravorty Spivak. Baltimore, London: Johns Hopkins University Press, 1997 (corrected edition).

de Saussure, Ferdinand. 1916. *Course in general linguistics*. Translated from French by Roy Harris, La Salle, Ill.: Open Court, 1983.

Eisenman, Peter. 1995. *Aura und Exzess: Zur Überwindung der Metaphysik der Architektur. Essays und Gespräche 1976–1994*. Vienna: Passagen Architektur.

Loos, Adolf. 2009. *Warum die Architektur keine Kunst ist*. Reprint Vienna: Metroverlag.

Popper, Karl. 1934/1959. *The Logic of Scientific Discovery*. London, New York: Routledge. Original published in German in 1934; first English translation in 1959.

VI Social Media and the Ecology of Emotion

Celebrities are the new class of attention super-rich that media society has given rise to. Celebrity culture, its upper-class affiliation notwithstanding, is far from being just another variant of elitist culture. The new upper class is thoroughly different from the long-established propertied class that Pierre Bourdieu not so long ago described as the upper class (see Bourdieu 1979). Celebrity culture, in contrast to old elitist high culture, is neither pronouncedly distinguished nor demonstratively highbrow. You can become a celebrity just by being seen with the right people in the right surroundings. In the eyes of media celebrities, it is regarded as sinfully snobbish not to be popular with the masses. For them, such selectiveness would mean to defraud themselves of the highest possible reward, namely their popularity.

Celebrity culture, accordingly, is far from the superior composure of classical high culture. It is a culture of fashion, not of elegance. Fashion is quick, eye-catching and novelty ridden; elegance is exclusive and reserved. Elegance is a luxury that those scrambling for attention in the world of mass attraction can hardly afford. In celebrity culture, elegance assumes a distinctly old-fashioned tone. It finds itself replaced by a less reserved and less discreet alternative: glamour. Glamour is what remains of elegance after subtracting elegant restraint. Glamour can be noisy, lusty, showy, shrill: it can, in short, be anything raising competitiveness in the struggle for attention. Elegance cannot. Celebrity culture, therefore, is good news for fashion, but bad news for elegance.

The Most Innovative Drug Market

One of the remarkable innovations in the symbolism of the 'upper' upper class, is that celebrity culture awaits popularization. In the media themselves, formats such as casting and reality shows have been introduced for disseminating the message to the masses that anybody can become a celebrity. The popularity of these formats, produced relatively cheaply since professional actors and elaborate scripts are not

G. Franck, *Vanity Fairs*,
https://doi.org/10.1007/978-3-030-41532-7_7

required, testifies that the new edition of the story of the dishwasher's ascension to millionaire found a willing audience. The message of staging ordinary people in a TV show performed a translation into popular culture famously practiced by the avant-gardists—epitomized by Marcel Duchamp's exhibition of a urinal in an art show—demonstrating that it is not the outstanding quality, but simply the frame of the presentation that qualifies the exhibit as a piece of art. The genre arising from this translation is that of the aforementioned reality show. Reality shows demonstrate that nothing more is needed for creating celebrity, however short-lived it may be, than being made to appear in a frame such as television.

Reality TV, however, is not the end of the popularization or socialization of celebrity. It means, rather, that celebrity culture follows that pattern of the socialization of erstwhile luxuries. Social media, the latest edition of advertising-financed new media, is a minor technological innovation that has been turned into a major booster of social change by simply downscaling the business model of mass media. Social media are mass media downscaled to the level of retail or, rather, the vendor's tray. Everybody can now engage in creating a media hype, be it by uploading a smartphone video on Youtube, disseminating a conspiracy theory on Facebook, or posting some intriguing fake news on Twitter, if only the number and growth rate of page views are noticed. The success of social media is much less due to content than to the inclination of people to pay attention to what others pay attention to. Everything that conspicuously attracts attention assumes attractiveness on the part of even those that are largely uninterested in the content as such.

Facebook, Instagram, Twitter & co. rely on minor technological innovations since interactivity and the possibility of online publication are as old as the internet itself. Two innovations are remarkable, however. The first concerns the placement of ads and is due to Google; the second consists of the downscaling of the business model of mass media, including the measurement of the attention cashed in. Google got ahead of its competitors early on due not only to its superior search engine technology (keyword: PageRank[1]), but also by virtue of its way of dealing with ads. Google was the first supplier of information services that reacted to the nuisance factor of ads (a

[1]PageRank (Brin and Page 1998), the algorithm that the superior performance of Google's search engine relies on, translates the model of citation indexing (SCI) into a general purpose system of indexing the information accessible by web addresses, helped by gigantic data centres constantly indexing the web. The crucial difference to the academic citation system lies in the ranking of hypertext pages. Incoming links are not just counted but weighed (normalized) according to the number of links on the page. This means that a link coming from a node with a high rank has more weight than a link coming from a node with low rank. By thus accounting for the unequal distribution of incoming attention and the upward bias that wealth gives rise to in its valuation, the apparently flat data ocean of the internet is made to show dynamic hierarchies according to the visibility and importance of each website (cf. Pasquinelli 2009, p. 4). Contrary to traditional mass media and neophyte social media, Google does not produce any content itself. It thus keeps the algorithm free of contamination from marketing interests. The only quasi-contents Google Search produces are the service of the search engine itself and the user data falling incidentally into its lap. The attention the service attracts and the user data gathered are marketed on the separate advertisement platform AdWords, which will be addressed later in this chapter. It is the insatiable demand of the ad industry for these secondary services on which Google's frightening business power relies.

factor verified by the popularity of ad blockers). It started utilizing the data entered by the user to contextualize advertisement (keyword: AdWords). Users searching e.g. for music lessons or painting courses are most probably disinterested in offers from banks or hotels. Someone typing in "mortgage" or "wellness", in contrast, might very well be susceptible to such offers. Thus contextualized advertising not only treats the user's attention with care but also improves the service deliverable to the advertiser. The user data skimmed off can be sold as a service in itself, thus opening the new field of business mentioned above (p. 18f).

This field was tailor-made for social media, the invention of which was completed by another stroke of business acumen. To downscale the business model of mass media, including the measurement of the attention cashed in, currencies such as 'followers', 'friends' and 'likes' had to be introduced. It is only through currencies such as these that the user's revenue can be measured in the way citations measure the attention income of the publishing scientist or audience ratings measure the same for the performer on TV. The simple but striking idea of the inventors of social media was to thus translate *the personal bank account* into the economy of attention. The generalization of the market form of the vanity fair has reached an endpoint by turning every smartphone user into a participant. No earlier medium came so close to realizing the addiction potential of attention. Socialization of the privilege to work for the wage of fame, in combination with the monetization of user data, functions as a devilishly effective business model in the mixed economy of attention and money.

There are, to be sure, users of social media whose prime interest is just information or maintenance of contacts. Those addicted to Facebook, Twitter, Instagram and the like, however, are anxious to see their account of followers, friends and likes grow. What is so interesting about this account is that it shows the documented income of attention of the user. Immediately being shown the impact of one's publishing or messaging activity—that is the real kick of being present on Facebook, Instagram, Youtube & co.[2] The interest in updates and the maintenance of one's contacts is merely a perfect smokescreen for the greed for attention.

The force of this kick is demonstrated by the ease with which it overrides users' concerns of privacy violation. Users essentially allow the providers to spy on their private lives. Protection of privacy from prying eyes and ears—the fundamental right to privacy as such—has been one of the major issues in the ongoing battle for civil rights in the face of the 21st century's culture of widespread surveillance. Social media even allow the suppliers to trade with the data and to sell them to agencies that manufacture them into information services offered to employers, banks, health insurances, detective agencies etc.

[2]The priority of the 'kick' is even confirmed by empirical method. In a careful statistical analysis of Youtube user data, Huberman et al. (2009) measured the weight that attention income has as a motive to upload videos. They observed how each contributor responds to different amounts of attention received. Not only did they find a strong correlation between attention and productivity, but also went into the question of whether an increase of attention causes productivity or vice versa. By testing the direction of causality in terms of prediction accuracy, they could show that it is indeed attention that plays a determinant role in the productivity of those uploading videos. It is, in other words, not just productivity that earns attention, but the wage of fame that stimulates productivity.

In socializing the once exclusive privilege of artists and scientists to work for the wage of fame, social media go as far as fulfilling Andy Warhol's prophecy of the fifteen minutes of fame available to everybody. Youtube even socializes the privilege that Hollywood once could monopolize—namely the film industry's ability to launch unknowns on a stellar trajectory. The new class of stars are of the kind of the Youtuber managing to succeed in viral marketing, the influencer becoming a brand himself by cross-fading the brands advertised, or of the party girl finding herself turned into an it-girl due to the click rate of a snapshot on Instagram. To this new arena for the battle for attention everybody is admitted, and there they are free to publish whatever they like. The gatekeepers characteristic of old media have disappeared. Finally, you are allowed to fight for attention by whatever means, fair or foul.

Still, what the falling barriers to access have left unchanged is the unequal distribution of income and wealth. Material wealth continues to be obscenely unequally distributed, including the power to influence public opinion via lobbying. The distribution of public attention follows a steepening social gradient as well. It is not without reason, thus, that free access to publication was understood by those who feel neglected and passed over as encouragement to give expression to their bad feelings. A topic that quickly gained traction on social media is the now seemingly ubiquitous anger against the elites. This excitement, remarkably, is not just a widespread form of frustration and criticism, but a highly specific and indeed novel form of organized protest. The tumult we are witnessing in the realm of social media is unprecedented insofar as it has left the sphere of material economy and moved to the level of the economy of attention, which in turn has been transposed into a global economy by the worldwide web of digital technology. Today, the desire for revenge is sweeping the internet. Media and social networks create and enhance unlimited emotional upheaval, poking at the wounds of the disaffected, and encouraging all those feeling disadvantaged for whatever reasons to take revenge on societal relations by unleashing avalanches of aggressive insults, indignation and hatred. The complaints of the disadvantaged are no longer restricted to the disproportion of the share of wages and profits in the social product, but extend to the disproportion of public attention shared between the 'elites' and the 'people'. Does it make sense to assume that the inequality in the social distribution of attention has reached a pain threshold that makes the neglected and forgotten rebel in masses? Are we witnessing a hunger revolt of starving self-esteem?

The Synergetic Potential of Vanity and Resentment

Let us venture a charitable interpretation. Let us start with conceding the possibility of situations wherein pressure might be capable of turning a vice into a virtue. A hunger revolt is a case in point. In a hunger revolt of starving self-esteem, those rebelling are about to turn the value system inherent in the social gradient upside down. The prestige enjoyed by the better-off is turned into shame. The job of resentment, under these revolutionary conditions, is to perform the reversal individually. In the picture of the hunger revolt, the enraged citizen (*Wutbürger*) features as a sort of Robin Hood, teaching the impoverished and overlooked masses to turn the higher degrees of social status from something worthy of admiration into something worthy only of contempt. Resentment thus may appear as another means of exorcising the inclination to discriminate between attention from above and attention from below.

According to this charitable interpretation, the emotional climate change is the phase of proletarian dictatorship of a Marxian revolution transposed into the context of the capitalist economy of attention. As a revolution of this stature, it includes the promise of bringing forth a 'new man'. This new man's novelty relies on a thorough re-education—if not reconstitution—of evaluative self-awareness. Hence, not only the traditional appreciation of social status is turned on its head, but also the controlling function of direct self-respect is dismissed as such. Liberated from the straitjacket of self-respect, the ego is now free to switch between whatever standards of estimation it deems suitable for its own growth.

The emotional climate change we are witnessing bears traits of a proletarian dictatorship, to be sure. Never before have human emotions so eagerly and efficiently been multiplied and exploited for personal ego-enhancement, cheap thrills and indulgence in shared negativity by private netizens as well as political movements. In the media sphere, emotionalized hypes and, in particular, negative emotions spread as freely as climate pollutants (cf. Franck 2017). Nevertheless, the story of the hunger revolt is ultimately unconvincing. Even though there are thresholds of inequality where losers start to see red, it is hard to see why the number of losers should have exploded recently. It seems, rather, that a catalyst has recently been introduced which harbours the potential of boosting the power of resentment as a pain-reliever for even mild forms of dissatisfaction. What if resentment and vanity are strategies of ego-enhancement that are not only closely related, but potentially synergetic?

What if resentment is also good as a strategy for compensating for one's inability to raise the funds required by the ambition of one's self-esteem? Paying back the rejection one suffers in failing to persuade oneself and others that those denying recognition are themselves not worth respect includes the assignment of finding resonance. As pointed out in Chapter "Competition in the Service of Self-esteem", the strategy works only by finding allegiance. In a sense, thus, the denigrator finds himself back to square one: he still faces the task of earning attention—what has changed is just the target group. The new target group are those who themselves are in the business of denigration. Since the task of finding followers is essential to the business, the new target group tends to be quite lucrative. It includes all those who themselves use resentment as a pain-reliever for even minor forms of disappointment. It includes all those whose resentment is manifested by the preparedness to pay attention to whatever endorses it. To put it bluntly, the means for finding pain-relief includes the demand for news, rumours, half-truths, conspiracy theories—even full-blown lies—that give the appearance of confirming one's prejudices.

The Catalyst of the Synergy of Vanity and Resentment

Demand is only as effective as preparedness to pay for the item demanded. Today, the markets supplying resentment on an unprecedented scale are the media. As markets supplying resentment, the old media are of limited use. Press and book publishers are traditionally reluctant to supply the information and, in particular, disinformation that resentment demands. The press turned a blind eye to the concerns of the politically incorrect as long as it was under the purview of classical journalism. It belonged to the professional honour of the classical journalist to serve the audience with objectivity and reflection rather than trying to please the crowd. Things changed with new media, in which it is predominantly the attention measured in circulation figures, audience ratings and page views that counts. The triumph of advertising-financed media was connected to shifts in power between journalism, public relations and marketing, linked to a lasting loss of trust in journalism (cf. Fengler and Ruß-Mohl 2008). Where the service of attraction becomes more important than the production of news and reflected opinion, the vox populi also gets new opportunities to assert itself against journalistic virtue.

The advent of social media triggered a final, catastrophic breach in the dam which had, until then, restrained the mainstream of public opinion,. Not only did they leave the gatekeepers who were controlling the old media behind, they also made it possible to participate, with the help of nothing more than a smartphone, as both consumer and producer in a market where you can grow rich, for example, by uploading a fallacious story to Facebook if only it appeals to widespread prejudice. It is sufficient that the number and rate of increase of page views grow conspicuous; the details and consistency of the content are not so significant.

The way was thus paved for measurement of attention to replace the checking of facts. In this way, social media turned into a greenhouse for growing what resentment demands. The tendency of conspicuity to reinforce itself is particularly accommodating for resentment services. Since resentment is in its element only when finding resonance, it is loaded, on its own, with potential synergy. Where the readiness for indignation is widespread, only a single spark of affirmation is required to set off an inferno of aggressive insults, hatred, and defamation, which, once released, rush through the new media and engulf the already-weakened edifice of old media. Denigration, and the spreading of negative emotionality have blossomed into regular success recipes in the fight for followers and likes.

This perspective goes a long way to explaining how rambling frustration and media resonance coincide and how the use of resentment has become the dominant strategy of overgrown narcissists. With the aid of popular indignation and the promise of revenge against the arrogant elites, it is easy to harvest the masses of attention on which the overweening ego thrives. Even as a member of these elites, one can put the crown on one's vanity by slipping into the role of the leader of the storm of resentment against these same elites. Perhaps we are touching upon the reason why populist movements are so prone to cherish narcissistic leaders—a topic germane to our day and age, if not directly to this book.

The Economic Background of Emotional Climate Change

Instead of finding the assumption of the hunger revolt confirmed, we are on the track of a much more plausible explanation of the emotional climate change. What is looming before our eyes is a synthesis, catalysed by social media, of moments of resentment and vanity enforcing one another. We face resentment utilized as a strategy for satisfying the demand of vanity for attention. We see the double condemnation of vanity and resentment turned into a double invitation to a lucrative black market. By showing allegiance to the demand of resentment one can make a fortune with documented attention. Add as particular circumstances the retreat of the classical gatekeepers plus a public view of the elites that displays them as either unwilling, or even downright unable to show themselves worthy of the privileges they so conspicuously enjoy, and you will no longer wonder why it is just now that we face another climate change.

The business opportunities the economy of attention currently affords are more formidable than ever before. The attention economy itself has grown into the now standard business model of the media industries. Its latest innovation includes media consumption incorporated into the business model proper. Media consumption is no longer restricted to the consumption of the information delivered by the industry. Social media blur the difference between producer and consumer. Consumption now includes media use for the purpose of earning attention. Consumers consume what other consumers produce for getting their attention. The access barriers to the producer's market have practically vanished. The sweeping success of Facebook, Instagram, Twitter & co. testifies to the enormous demand for possibilities of earning attention, which, in turn, testifies to the significance of self-esteem as a motive of business behaviour. The attention measured in terms of page views, likes and followers corresponds to the social product measured in terms of money income. Along with the recent growth of the market, we should expect a growth of shadow markets at the same or even higher rate when one considers the new possibilities of hiding in anonymity and hiring bots for boosting disinformation.

The enhanced possibilities of disinformation put a new complexion on the accepted fact that the ego's appetite for attention knows no limits. It has never been so easy to complain about being denied the attention one thinks one deserves. It is no longer so important, thus, to ask whether one's frustration is due to the ignorance of others or to one's own overblown claims. As long as you don't feel privileged yourself, you can always find reasons to feel left out. It then depends firstly on the fragility of your self-respect, and secondly on the supply of opportunities for revenge, as to whether it pays to enter the resentment business. Why not seize the opportunity to blame others for your frustration if self-respect provides no bar to this easy way out? The business of slandering those you blame becomes lucrative as soon as you find an audience that shares your prejudice and the desire for signs of confirmation. The resonance thus stimulated is disposed to be reinforced by the intrinsic greed of resentment for acclaim. It then depends on the size and accessibility of the pertinent information markets as to whether everybody susceptible to resentment can be activated as clientele demanding your fiddle and disinformation.

To summarize: the synergetic potential of vanity and resentment makes it difficult to determine to what extent resentment and vanity respectively are responsible for exacerbating the normal occurrence of everyday malice in the ongoing emotional climate change. What is clear, however, is the role of media in activating the synergy. The penetration of the lifeworld with digital technology was connected with a breakthrough in the economization of attention. Interpersonal exchange of attention, insofar as mediated by technology, found itself transformed into a globalized market. An expanding market opens novel opportunities, both legitimate and fraudulent. Since the intersubjective exchange of attention is immediately connected to the intrasubjective conversion of esteem received into self-esteem, it was to be expected that the inner economy of self-esteem had to adapt to its novel environment. An unexpected side effect of the flexibility of the inner accounting system was the opening of a loophole awaiting detection by business acumen. Business acumen found out that resentment not only works as a salve with regards to starved self-esteem—but also as a means to improve the income on which the ordinary ego lives. It even found out that resentment, in the media sphere, is a business that lures with increasing returns to scale.

Towards an Ecology of Emotion

The returns to investment in defamation, however, are like those into deteriorating environmental resources. They add to the turnover of the numeraire but do not add to the value of the social product. They inflate the turnover in terms of money or attention but devalue the stock of resources that the quality of life depends on. The situation of the enraged citizen is like that of the executive in the fishing industry who invests in intensifying the overfishing of the oceans. For society, the net result of the investment is negative even though it may pay for the individual investor. The resource that the enraged citizen's investment depletes is the stock of trust and benevolence incorporated in the emotional condition of the members of society. How smoothly, comfortably and self-sufficiently the web of social interactions can work depends entirely on this stock. It is for the lifeworld's atmosphere what fresh air is for the physical atmosphere. In sociology, the stock is discussed under the title 'social capital'.[3] There is widespread consensus about the stock's being an indispensable condition for quality of social life.

---

[3]There are two concepts of social capital to be kept apart, the one introduced by Pierre Bourdieu, the other introduced by Robert D. Putnam. Bourdieu (1986) defines social capital as a sort of symbolic capital: the social relations that the owner utilizes as a means of distinction, i.e. of the enforcement of social distance. Putnam (1995) defines social capital as the stock of trust and benevolence as addressed here. When using the concept in this essay, I refer exclusively to Putnam's definition.

The stock, of course, has to do with but is not the same thing as the sum total of the esteem transported in the social exchange of attention. It manifests, rather, in the expectations that people derive from their experiences in this exchange. The stock's way of becoming productive (i.e. activated as a capital) lies in defining the *default of social interaction*. It depends on the standard expectation as to how civilized and convenient social intercourse is generally allowed to work; whether, for example, courtesy and cooperation or mistrust and deception are the rule to be reckoned with. By its very nature, the stock works as a dynamic and self-correlated whole. The expectations are not only derived from experience, but feed back into, and thus influence, what they condition. The stability conditions of the stock's dynamics are crucial in determining what the collective results of such defamation campaigns and organized movements fuelled by resentment will turn out to be. Stability in terms of dynamics means that what happens, happens again and again, and the effect of any disturbances tends to be dampened, thus securing the return of the process to its initial rhythm. Dynamic instability, in contrast, means that disturbances are reinforced instead of dampened, thus driving the process further and further away from its initial conditions. As long as the stock is robust enough to dampen any negative media hype, nothing particularly disruptive will happen. However as soon, as the resilience of the process is overstressed, the stock may degenerate towards collective hysteria and a lynching mood. Since defamation works to split up society into 'we, the (true) people', and 'those others' (be it migrants, Jews, elites or whoever are the suspects), a crucial condition of the stability of the stock lies in the relevant majority's resistance to being polarized into in-group and out-group. Or, insofar as this polarization is itself a by-product of spreading resentment, the condition of stability is that the relevant majority remains immune to the lures of resentment.

Conceived as a resource that is fundamental to quality of life and whose use feeds back into its productivity, the stock of trust and benevolence strongly resembles an environmental resource. In fact, it is the ecology in which the economy of attention is embedded. It embeds, firstly, the individual participants as embodied psyches, who, secondly, embody the social context in turn. Even though instantiated individually, this stock of trust and benevolence works as a whole, thus differing from the economic concept of capital. In economics, capital denotes the class of pre-produced means of production suited to enhance productivity and capable of being privately owned and thus traded and priced on markets. In contrast to economic capital, social capital resists being parcelled into private property. Its nature, rather, is that of a *commons*. It is a community good, accessible to anybody. Nobody can be excluded from its use even if this use inflicts serious damage to the resource. The gain from using the commons, as epitomized by the business of resentment, can be appropriated individually, whereas the costs are born collectively. This asymmetry between individual gain and social cost is what economic theory refers to in distinguishing economy and ecology.

In the context of attention economy, the splitting up of economy and ecology has only recently been addressed explicitly. Yves Citton, pioneering the ecology of attention (Citton 2017), raised the overdue question about the 'climate change' that the lifeworld generally undergoes in the wake of mental capitalism. What effect does the penetration of the lifeworld with digital and, in particular, attraction technologies that attention finds itself arbitrarily dealing with have on this environment? What does it mean that the contents that constitute our consciousness by way of its intentionality are increasingly mediated by media run by business interests, serving user interests only for reasons of profit maximization? By extending lines of thought initiated by theorists such as Jonathan Craig, Jonathan Beller, Catherine Hayles and Bernard Stiegler, Citton outlines a climate change that continually pushes attention to new extremes of a Janus-faced capitalism which simultaneously advocates relentless productive discipline and limitless consumerist hedonism. Yves Citton's concept of climate change thus predominantly, if not exclusively, concerns those tendencies to alienation that are due to rules of commercialization imposed on the working of vanity fairs from outside. It highlights phenomena such as attention deficit hyperactivity disorder (ADHD), the acceleration in communication, new media apparatuses and information overload, but only incidentally overlaps with the concept of social capital, endangered from within the psychic households. Both notions of climate change, nevertheless, are united in focusing on the depth effect that media technologies have on the energy balances of psychic households. The energies accessible by supplying news, distraction, thrills and entertainment—in short, by addressing vanity and resentment—were hedged against excessive forms of exploitation as long as access relied on less pervasive and less invasive technologies of attraction. Before the advent of new media, the ecology of attention was as secure as rainforests were before the introduction of chainsaws, as oceans were before ground trawling, as the atmosphere was before combustion engines. As long as the exchange of attention was restricted to face-to-face contacts, it was very improbable that resentment could become epidemic. Before it could endanger the stock of trust and benevolence, it was dampened by the resilient default of interpersonal relations with their proven practices of nudging and encouragement to relaxation. There were, to be sure, catastrophic events in history such as civil wars and sweeping ideologies that in fact corroded the stock of social capital. In the civilized lifeworld of democratic societies, however, the established management of the social-emotional commons was close to being naturally sustainable in pre-digital times. Consumption and regeneration of the stock were roughly in balance.

Things changed with the latest thrust of innovation—or, rather with its advent coinciding with a particularly destabilizing phase of globalization: of unpredictable terrorist violence, of wars fought by irate fundamentalists and cold Machiavellians, where avalanches of aggressive insults, indignation and emotional manipulation by sensationalist media and populist parties became as inevitable as bad weather.

Ecologically, the introduction of social media corresponds to that of motor cars. From now on your Facebook or Twitter account can individually consume the service of common trust and benevolence much like your heavily emissive SUV can consume, without contributing to regeneration, the absorptive and regenerative powers of the atmosphere. You can appropriate the gain from the use individually while the costs you individually cause are borne collectively. This asymmetry of individual gain and social cost is the economic base of the resentment business. Why not join this business of turning your personal frustration into global opprobrium by simply appealing to those who share similar frustrations to you? Why not? There are no disincentives: you will not be made accountable for the costs of your damage to the emotional commons.

What we thus face is a "tragedy of the commons" as exemplified in the seminal article by Garret Hardin. Hardin (1968) points out that commons, be it the medieval village pastures, fishable waters or irrigation systems, are doomed to ruin themselves since it pays individually to overgraze (up to the point where average cost distributed individually equals individual gain: the mark of the final destruction of the resource). It is only by restricting free access and levying costs that disaster can be fended off. Regarding the emotional commons, this would mean to impose a kind of environmental tax on detrimental forms of media use (an idea that may not be totally crazy since the levy promises to be fiscally fertile). However, nobody abhorring dictatorship can welcome an authority that distinguishes harmless from detrimental forms of media use.

It is comforting, thus, to learn that Hardin's requiem on the commons was countered by the first woman to win the Nobel prize in economics. Elinor Ostrom showed both empirically and analytically that the management of commons is a mode of production potentially superior to both privately owned and government-managed means of production (Ostrom 1990). Among the examples of working commons are Swiss alpine pastures, Turkish inland fisheries, countless irrigation systems and the freshwater basins of Los Angeles. Ostrom very clearly points out that the condition of maintaining and successfully operating commons lies in the ability of the community to deal with those perverse incentives to overuse the resource.

The emotional commons of trust and benevolence is as indispensable to civilized society as are clean air and freshwater to healthy life. It is no option, thus, to witness its spoliation indifferently. Nor is it to be expected that the causes of the emotional warm-up will dissolve by themselves. The ongoing hazards, rather, will bring problems for many, and for most will entail a shift away from the comfort zone. We face changes for which we are unprepared, because they require more than mere technical adjustments. To meet the challenges, we need reflection and research that focus, without reservations, on the question of how the perverse incentives to run down the social ecology can be overcome.

We are back to the question of how to translate into action the criticism of the commercial transformation of attention economy. Inclusion of the ecological dimension confirms, however, that the prospects of regulatory policies are poor. It will hardly be possible to suppress emotional pollution by legal measures without slipping into sorts of censorship, which in their own turn inflict damage on the emotional commons. It certainly makes sense to think about reshaping the media infrastructure beyond narrowly targeted state intervention. The first condition, however, that any reform has to satisfy, is the promise of dampening the impulse to overuse the emotional commons. The problem with this condition is that it does not first of all address media infrastructure, but emotional self-regulation. The basic question thus is whether human emotionality is disposed to deal with the economic rationalization of its inner household, or whether it is overstrained by the thrust of rationalization as imposed by the recent self-development of the social economy of attention.

The pessimistic answer is much more in line with the zeitgeist than considering ethics as a resource of empowerment. In order to take that answer seriously let us reconsider those suspicions, addressed at the end of Chapter "Competition in the Service of Self-esteem", that the very construction of emotional self-regulation suffers from a disastrous design flaw.

Re-engineering Instinctive Emotionality?

The energies behind the emotional warm-up have been set free rather than originally generated by the latest media innovation. These energies, if our analysis is halfway correct, have their common origin in self-esteem's dependency on recognition. Might it thus be that we were too quick in dismissing the suspicions of those hermits and ascetics that the dependency of self-esteem is a dysregulation in our naturally evolved emotionality that waits to be overcome?

We were too quick insofar as the suspicion has made its way from the hermitage to Silicon Valley, taking root in the think tanks run by those new media corporations. The new doctrine of salvation is called transhumanism and claims that humanity is waiting for self-redemption by way of genetic optimization, nanotechnology and supplanting human with artificial intelligence. Transhumanists proclaim that our instinct-based, naturally evolved emotionality is suboptimal and obsolete. They think that cost-benefit analyses of emotional self-regulation are viable and indeed capable of being translated into technological projects (see Spiekermann et al. 2017).

The prospect of a radical improvement of the cognitive powers and moral character through genetic engineering and artificial intelligence has led transhumanists such as Eliezer Yudkowsky to advocate that humanity submit self-governance to more enlightened successors. Yudkowsky, like other evangelists of a coming artificial intelligence 'singularity',[4] believes that human cognitive limitations will quickly be superseded by the super-rationality of a recursively self-improving artificial intelligence, unconstrained by biology and evolutionary drives. Human brains, he argues, will never have the kind of capacity for self-improvement and perfect rationalization that machine minds will have, namely 'total read/write access to their own state', the ability to 'absorb new hardware', 'understandable code', 'modular design', and a 'clean internal environment' (Yudkowsky 2008). In fact, argues Yudkowsky, human cognition is so irredeemably constrained by bias, and our motivations so driven by aggression and self-interest, that we should give up on the project of self-governance through rational debate and instead do our best to hasten the day when we can turn our affairs over to a super-rational artificial intelligence programmed to act in our best interests (cf. Hughes 2010).

Once the use of media becomes essential to the completion of our every daily task, the residual user data in the global networks will enable a super-AI to intuit the

[4]Singularity, in the context of AI, denotes the historical moment when artificial surpasses human intelligence. See Kurzweil (2005).

desires and needs of all human beings and make the decisions necessary to satisfy them. Any objection to being ruled by this enlightened AI is based on anthropocentric projections of the fallibility of human despotism. As Michael Anissimov explains, enlightened AI despotism will be completely trustworthy. In fact, he suggests, only godlike AI, built from pure code and free of evolved Darwinian behaviours and programmed, instead, for human friendliness, can be trusted as a global totalitarian controlling power:

> The fear of patriarchy objection stems largely from history, wherein all of the relevant actors were members of our unique species, for which power is proven to corrupt. Power corrupts humans for evolutionary reasons—if one is on top of the heap, one had better take advantage of the opportunity to reward one's allies and punish one's enemies. This is pure evolutionary logic and need not be consciously calculated. AIs, which can be constructed entirely without selfish motivations, can be immune to these tendencies. Insofar as significant power asymmetries in general bother people, this seems hard to avoid in the long term technological development will lead to a diversity of possible beings, and with this diversity will inevitably come a diversity in levels of capability and intelligence. (Anissimov 2007)

A super-AI will be capable not only of monitoring media use, as does the NSA, but also to interfere and intervene therapeutically. It could be taught—or teach itself—to manage the stability of the dynamics of the emotional commons. It is even conceivable that such a system might dedicate itself exclusively to constraining those perverse incentives to overuse the invaluable resource. This would be the prolongation of what legislators are currently considering to combat defamation and disinformation in media use. Regarding the influence that transhumanists have gained and the research funds going into AI, such a project may not be pure fantasy. What is so disconcerting, when considering thoughts such as these, is that the protection of the emotional commons becomes indistinguishable from its abolition. If the maintenance of the ecology is granted automatically, the stock of trust and benevolence is made insensitive to the experience of the people. It is like supplanting weather with global air conditioning. For robots born of robots, this may be perfectly ok. For embodied souls, however, this is a nightmare. They find their emotional self-regulation overruled by machine-made conditioning.

True, the fear of finding one's self-regulation overruled 'stems largely from history, wherein all of the relevant actors were members of our unique species, for which power is proven to corrupt'. But what about the possibility that self-learning machine minds that have 'total read/write access to their own state' get corrupted? Systems such as these have access also to their own objective function, i.e. the function instructing their decisions and plans. There is no guarantee that such a system never comes up with the idea of manipulating this function with the result of degenerating into malignancy.[5] Even disregarding corruption, however, the fear of finding one's self-regulation overruled stems not only from history's lesson. The feeling of

[5] Witness the chatbot Tay that was developed by Microsoft to 'experiment with and conduct research on conversational understanding'. It happened, however, that the robot got into contact with hate postings, and misogynistic and racist remarks. And Tay—supposed to learn to engage people through 'casual and playful conversation'—started repeating these sentiments back to users. It did not even balk at variations on 'Hitler was right' or '9/11 was an inside job', thus forcing Microsoft to apologize

being overruled by a foreign intelligence is deadly, above all, for the sense of self. You are no longer responsible for your deeds, nor can your conspecifics be made responsible for theirs. A constellation is engendered whereby mediated self-esteem is disavowed and also unmediated self-respect no longer has much say.

Critics of instinctive, biology-driven emotionality may see thus outlined a strategy for exorcising the plague of narcissism. Instead of having purified emotional self-regulation, however, both object and subject of self-love would be erased. The exorcism would amount to a final brainwash—a brainwash that converts its victims to the belief of being nothing but robots born of robots born of robots. Even a godlike AI, built from pure code, will be of robotic nature and thus perfectly free of phenomenal states. There is no idea whatsoever of how to produce phenomenal states by way of computation. It is pretty clear, on the contrary, that 'what it is like' feelings are non-algorithmic. Hence, can the transhumanists be serious at all when claiming they feel themselves to be robots? Isn't the claim paradoxical and thus self-defeating? As soon as there is a feeling of being something, there is no longer mere information processing, but also a subject that is mentally present. The paradox notwithstanding, we cannot dismiss the possibility of feeling ourselves to be a robot. The reason is that it is indeed easy to forget that there is a feeling of being the being one is. We, as unavoidably sentient beings, are so familiar with this feeling that it needs explicit self-awareness to become aware of its existence. Once you have realized, however, that you exist not only as a living body, but as a psyche whose mode of existence is mental presence, you are unable to feel like a robot any longer. You are unable, in particular, to confuse the processing of your personal data in some information-processing capacity with the reception of psychic attention. Since the pursuit of attention lies at the foundations of the main industry of knowledge society as well as of the business models of those new media corporations, we collectively testify the non-robotic nature of our species.

For the psyche, it makes no sense to speculate about adopting a robotic nature. For a psyche that feels mentally present, thinking about replacing the existence of a sentient being with a machinic vision of information-processing capabilities amounts to playing with the idea of suicide. Nor does it make sense to think about re-engineering emotionality as if it were just a bundle of objective functions implemented in some information-processing capacity. The solution space of the ecological problem, rather, finds itself whittled down to the management of emotional self-regulation. We have to identify attitudes and habitual patterns of behaviour that are ripe for and susceptible to re-education. We have to find ethical principles independent of religious or philosophical adherence, principles that allow coexistence on a shrinking planet.

---

in public and to cancel the experiment. https://www.theguardian.com/technology/2016/mar/24/tay-microsofts-ai-chatbot-gets-a-crash-course-in-racism-from-twitter (retrieved on 7.7.2017).

On concerns about the possibility of degenerating super-intelligence see Bostrom (2014).

References

Anissimov, Michael. 2007. *Objections to Coherent Extrapolated Volition*. Singularity Institute for Artificial Intelligence.

Bostrom, Nick. 2014. *Superintelligence: Paths, Dangers, Strategies*. Oxford: Oxford University Press.

Bourdieu, Pierre. 1979. *Distinction: A Social Critique of the Judgement of Taste*. Trans. Richard Nice. Cambridge, Mass.: Harvard University Press, 1984.

Bourdieu, Pierre. 1986. The Forms of Capital. In *Handbook of Theory and Research for the Sociology of Education*, ed. John G. Richardson, 241–258. New York: Greenwood Press.

Brin, Sergey, and Lawrence Page. 1998. *The Anatomy of a Large-Scale Hypertextual Web Search Engine*. http://infolab.stanford.edu/backrub/google.html.

Citton, Yves. 2017. *The Ecology of Attention*. Trans. From French by Barnaby Norman. Cambridge, UK, Malden, MA: Polity Press.

Fengler, Susanne, and Stephan Ruß-Mohl. 2008. Journalists and the Information-Attention Markets: Towards an Economic Theory of Journalism. *Journalism*, 2008—http://journals.sagepub.com.

Franck, Georg. 2017. Resonanz und Ressentiment (resonance and resentment), in: NZZ dated 6.2.2017, no. 30, p. 8 (International edition dated 7.2.2017, p. 17)

Hardin, Garrett. 1968. The Tragedy of the Commons. *Science* 162: 1243–1248.

Huberman, Bernardo A., Daniel M. Romero, and Wu Fang. 2009. Crowdsourcing, Attention and Productivity. *Journal of Information* 35 (6): 758–765.

Hughes, J. 2010. *Problems of Transhumanism: Liberal Democracy vs. Technocratic Absolutism*. Institute for Ethics and Emerging Technologies. https://ieet.org/index.php/IEET2/print/3670.

Kurzweil, Ray. 2005. *The Singularity is Near: When Humans Transcend Biology*. New York et al.: Penguin.

Ostrom, Elinor. 1990. *Governing the Commons: The Evolution of Institutions of Collective Action*. Cambridge: Cambridge University Press.

Pasquinelli, Matteo. 2009. Google's PageRank Algorithm: A Diagram of the Cognitive Capitalism and the Rentier of the Common Intellect. In Deep Search: The Politics of Search Beyond Google, eds. Konrad Becker, and Felix Stalder. London: Transaction Publishers, 2009.

Putnam, Robert D. 1995. Bowling Alone: America's Declining Social Capital. *Journal of Democracy* 6: 64–78.

Spiekermann, Sarah, Mark Coeckelbergh, Charles M. Ess, Georg Franck, Peter Hampson, and Johannes Hoff. 2017. The Ghost of Transhumanism & the Sentience of Existence. In *Research-Gate Technical Report*. https://www.researchgate.net/publication/318377886_The_Ghost_of_Transhumanism_the_Sentience_of_Existence.

Yudkowsky, Eliezer. 2008. Artificial Intelligence as a Positive and Negative Factor in Global Risk. In *Global Catastrophic Risks*, ed. Nick Bostrom, and Milan M. Ćirković, 308–345. New York: Oxford University Press.

VII Moral Elegance: An Ethics Tailored to Vanity Fairs?

Vanity fairs are the most successful market form of the 21st century economy. They represent the market form that the industrial base of knowledge society and the business models of the most prosperous firms of the present-day economy rely on. The success, however, comes at a price. Competitions for attention, incomparable in mobilizing creative and cognitive efforts, are incomparable also in exposing the tender flesh of our innermost selves to the cunning of business acumen. Hence the telltale salesmanship, manipulation and self-marketing in the service of self-esteem. Hence the perverse incentives to exploit the emotional commons.

It is tempting to read the dark side of the success story as symptomatic of a fateful mismatch between economic rationality and emotional self-regulation. The invitation is suggested by the association of economic rationality with utility maximization. This association, though disputed in economic theory proper, is all too easily translated into the economy of attention. Replace utility with self-esteem and you face a novel kind of homo economicus: the ego seeking to maximize attention income for maximizing self-esteem. The success story, by highlighting mass attraction and enrichment, favours this easy translation. Mass attraction is preoccupied with quantity and thus measurement; Matthew effectiveness is the silver bullet for enrichment.

In a sense, of course, the ego determined to grow rich in order to grow great in self-regard is a caricature, like the aforementioned homo oeconomicus. When looked at as a lodestar of emotional self-regulation, the sense of self-esteem appears as the most comprehensive inner guide for the individual's way of life. Its manner of orientation is the soft power of a libidinally tuned, multiply mediated, socially networked emotion. The keynote of self-esteem is affection, but the reference of the self-affection is broken by a change of perspective through which the self looks at itself as if from outside. This distanced look, however, accounts for more than the self's dependence on the affection of others: it accounts, at the same time, for the autonomy of the subject asking 'how do I stand in front of myself?' Self-esteem, to put it differently, requires success in both acquiring outer esteem and in feeling oneself to be one's own master. You have to manage the dependency in such a way

G. Franck, *Vanity Fairs*,
https://doi.org/10.1007/978-3-030-41532-7_8

that you are held in high esteem by others, as well as by your critical self. Hence the dualism of unmediated self-respect and mediated self-esteem.

The rigorous maximizer, though useful for illustrating the furore of commercialization, falls short of economic rationality in crucial respects. Utility, to start with, is not to be taken as a quantity whose maximization is the very definition of the pursuit of happiness—but is conclusively defined by way of an ordering of world states according to one's preference structure.[1] This ordering has to do only contingently with the maximization of quantifiable parameters. It means, rather, that efficiency in the pursuit of self-esteem, when defined comprehensively and consistently, has of course to do justice to the aesthetic, moral and spiritual dimensions of the feeling of being oneself. It requires that the very best is made of the interplay of self-interest and social dependency.

Instead of facing a fateful mismatch between economic rationality and emotional self-regulation, we see a gap opening between ideal-type efficiency and real-type business effectiveness. It is this gap that casts the shadow over that success story. Or is it rather that the success story could only thrive in its shade?

To answer this question, a critical assessment of the career of vanity fairs is not enough; criticism without considering what a feasible alternative might be risks culminating in mere complaint. What, accordingly, would an implementation of ideal-type efficiency in the pursuit of attention amount to? The question addresses self-esteem as that which motivates the pursuit in the last analysis. Is there something like an ideal-typical model economy of self-worth?

The question is too delicate to be confronted head-on. Let us first take the alternative model of economy into consideration, on which we touched in passing in the introduction—namely the option of general economy as theorized by Marcel Mauss and Georges Bataille. General economy is definitely humanities-minded, thus predisposed, as it seems, for theorizing an economy that is much more intuitive and aware of inner life than the explicitly calculation-and-efficiency-oriented concept of economy that standard economics entertains. General economy subordinates enrichment to generosity, outwitting in exchange to showering with gifts, investment to sovereign expenditure. Wealth of attention, according to general economy, is no end in itself, but a way of winning sovereignty and thus of self-aggrandizement by elegance and noblesse. Sovereign self-aggrandizement is a wishful dream rarely addressed in orthodox economic thought, but not at all alien to that inner economy of self-worth that of course accounts for the aesthetic, moral and spiritual dimension of self-regard.

General economy puts a new complexion on the economy of self-worth. Instead of being outpaced by business effectiveness, the claims of self-esteem overburden the efficiency of computational rationality. Self-esteem is not merely a question of social proof, just as social proof is not simply a question of what others think of us. In the judgement of ourselves, unmediated self-respect has a say as well, and the relevance of other people's opinion is weighted according to our own opinion of them. In both respects we are autonomous and only answerable to our own claims.

[1]The classic reference to this ordinal utility theory, as it is called, is de Graaff (1957).

In both respects, taste and moral sentiments are involved. Taste, to underscore the point, is much more than an arbitrary bundle of individual preferences and aversions: it is, if properly developed, the organ of sensuous intelligence. Moral sentiments are constitutive of self-respect and the sympathies we have of others as well. It is up to us how high we set their demands. It may sound a bit pretentious to call this freedom sovereignty, but it is quite appropriate for highlighting that ideal-type efficiency in the promotion of self-worth crosses over into perfection in personality formation.

General economy, nevertheless, is too cavalier with regard to the difficulty of balancing the weight of mediated self-esteem and unmediated self-regard. It underestimates the significance of social proof in the constitution of self-worth. Sovereign self-aggrandizement risks mutating into megalomania if it fails to find the delicate balance between autonomy and dependence. This balance is delicate indeed. It requires a distancing from oneself without losing the poise of one's autonomy, a somewhat acrobatic exercise when accounting for the impending contradiction of autonomy and dependence. It would be simply a misnomer to call the mastering of this exercise 'sovereignty'. True, mastering the balance has to do with sovereignty; but it has to do as well with uprightness, chivalry, honour and grace. You may include these old-fashioned virtues within sovereignty, but that does not suffice to give appropriate expression to what the sense of self-esteem entertains as its own ideal. It only feeds the suspicion that there is a ferment of elitism inherent in the ideal that the sense of self-esteem entertains as its constitutive goal.

The ferment of elitism, remarkably, is not imported by the claim of autonomy, but by the inevitable social dependence of what we are allowed to think of ourselves. The involuntary account for the payer's income in the valuation of the attention we receive establishes an upward bias that no argument in favour of egalitarianism can explain away. To re-emphasize, it is the scientific community, claiming to be unrivalled in mustering enlightened rationality, that has been the hotbed of Matthew effectiveness. Accounting for the upward bias must not be confused with justifying this reinforcement of natural inequality or with accepting it as a necessary evil. It means, rather, that one has to deal with the inevitable in a way that detoxifies the bias. This bias can surely be alleviated by such antidotes as empathy and respect. In order to give the ideal of self-esteem a more appropriate expression, sovereignty should be replaced with dignity.

Dignity sounds old-fashioned, too. But it is hard to find an alternative notion that gathers all those moments of high-mindedness, poise, morality, entitlement and grace that synthesize when the interplay of self-interest and social dependency convincingly succeeds. Nor is there something wrong with the idealist overtones of the accord. We are just looking to give expression to the ideal that the sense of self-esteem entertains out of its own logic. It is only logical, thus, that dignity puts us on the right track to a body of literature which gives, by philosophizing the pursuit of self-esteem, an aptly crafted expression of the price that had to be paid to mobilize the forces behind that success story. The track leads us—unexpectedly, but with good reason—to the origins of philosophical ethics.

The reference to ethics for pointing out why that success story could thrive only in the shadow may seem a strange detour, considering the notorious problems ethics has with its implementation. Ethics, as does economy, concerns the relation between individual and community. Economy reigns where equivalence of sacrifice and reward is the rule. Ethics is infamous for demanding more than it rewards. Upholding virtue, though good for the community, entails privation for the individual. The problem that ethics has with motivation comes to light in its notorious appeals to such concepts as duty or categorical imperatives, if not promises of otherworldly reward.

Towards a Secular Ethics

Self-esteem, ideally, does not demand more than it rewards. It is a goal in itself, worth being pursued for its own sake. In the case that the asymmetry of sacrifice and reward is not just an empirical regularity but constitutive for ethics, a secular ethics founded on self-esteem would be a contradiction in terms. The question thus becomes one of philosophical ethics. Is the lack of intrinsic motivation constitutive of ethics as such? An affirmative answer would imply that philosophical ethics has had to rely on external support from the very beginning. Remarkably, though, and fortunately also, philosophical ethics did not start with higher commands or social norms. The founding fathers of philosophical ethics were concerned much more with the redefinition of comforts than with the overruling power of deliberative reason or religious belief. Neither Confucius (China, 505–479 BC) nor Aristotle (Greece, 384–322 BC) had metaphysical principles or religious moralities in mind. For both, ethics was the concern of noblemen who sought to prove themselves worthy of the privileges they enjoyed. Neither would ever have thought of preaching morals to 'little people'. The high standards were for the upper class.

Philosophical ethics thus started with the question with which we find ourselves confronted due to the upward bias in the valuation of attention: how can inequality be made bearable? The issue, though rarely addressed in philosophical ethics in the intervening years, has become highly topical in recent times. The now commonplace anger against the elites has its root in both the obscenely unequal distribution of the economic gains and losses of globalization and in the indifference on the part of its beneficiaries to show themselves worthy of the privileges they so conspicuously enjoy. Regarding the political agenda, enhancing distributive fairness—and this means furthering equality—is of course the primary concern. Since it is hopeless, however, to remove inequality altogether, making inequality bearable is a remaining ethical concern. And it is a concern that immediately relates to the causes of emotional pollution. Though far from being a sufficient reason, the anger against the elites was key in unleashing the emotional warm-up.

Instead of good and evil, Confucius thought in terms of noble and mean. 'The superior man has a dignified ease without pride. The mean man has pride without a dignified ease' (Analects, Chap. II) (Confucius 2009). 'The superior man is easy to serve and difficult to please.... The mean man is difficult to serve, and easy to please' (ibid. Chap. XXV). The difference between mean and noble, accordingly, was that between greed and elegant restraint. On a personal basis, it is that between a stressed and a relaxed economy of self-esteem; interpersonally it is that between an angular and a fluent management of social relations. The superior man understands how to turn indebtedness and generosity into grace, the mean man demeans himself for small advantage. Ease, the state of effortless naturalness or undisturbed equilibrium of the soul, relates the tension between the common good and the pursuit of individual interest to one's embodiment of social context. To be at ease means to be in a 'flow'- or 'coherence'—like mode of embodying one's context: a mode occurring in, but not restricted to, meditative and creative practices.

Confucius, though sharing the concern of mindfulness with Buddha, was not Buddhist. Ease—the state of effortless naturalness or undisturbed equilibrium of the soul—is the distinguishing feature of the noble character. Noblesse of character is an end in itself; dismissing it knowingly and willingly amounts to self-contempt. The noble man, as envisioned by Confucius, is as far from the cynic as he is from the indiscriminately charitable who sacrifices himself for others. Rather he will take to heart the advice of the unconventional Buddhist teacher Chögyam Trungpa, that compassion has to be distinguished from idiot compassion. You have to be clear about what you can change and what you have to take as it is; what to consider as genuine help and what to rate as moral condescension. Submit to what you cannot change. It is idiotically compassionate to insist that inequality has to be removed instead of made bearable. It makes perfect sense to be concerned with reducing inequality, but you have to be aware of the trade-off between equality and freedom as well as the reasons why endeavours of enforcing egalitarianism have notoriously failed. Most of all, insisting that inequality has to be removed instead of made bearable is more a cheap excuse for defeatism than a call-to-liberation struggle. In short, morality has to be clearly distinguished from moral haughtiness.

To be sure, the intriguing charm of the noble character does not rely on moral imperturbability alone or even in the first place. What renders it so intriguing is the aesthetic appeal of dignified ease. The aesthetic appeal of the noble character moves even further to the centre in Aristotle's first approach to ethics as a philosophical subject. In his Eudemian Ethics (which probably predates the canonical Nicomachean Ethics) he conceptualizes the noble as *kalokagathía*, which literally translates as 'beauty and goodness': the coincidence of the aesthetically beautiful with the morally good (Aristotle 2011). Noblesse is the elegant appearance from the vantage point of moral honesty: the aesthetic appearance of moral goodness. To modern ears, this equation of aesthetically beautiful and morally good sounds hopelessly idealistic if not downright naive. For the ancient Greeks, it was only natural to see the good in the beautiful. *Kalokagathía*, as they called the overlap, unites sensual and moral elegance, which both commit the aesthetics to a standard of dignity and connect the elegant to the noble. And, lo and behold, the Greeks demonstrated how this bridging succeeds with perfect grace. Greek sculpture, tirelessly imitated but never surpassed, embodies perfect mastery of the ideal of second order naturalness . The fascination with this sculpture, continuing to this day, lies in the perfect obviousness that it gave to the idea of *kalokagathía*. The Greek sense of the manifestations of noblesse was admired beyond classical Greece since Roman times and was adopted as a model which was ultimately definitive for Western culture. It inspired a kind of reinvention that ultimately became perhaps the most significant export of English culture: the gentleman ideal.

The Gentleman[2] Ideal

The gentleman ideal concerns making inequality bearable from above, on the part of the privileged. Moreover, and in particular, it is an ideal whose plea for realization does not appeal to 'duty' or 'imperatives', much less even 'to moral obligation as routinely enforced by third party expressions of negative emotions' (Peil 2012, p. 24). It is an ideal worth being sought for its own sake. It is an elitist ideal, to be sure, and rarely invoked to flatten the social gradient. Nevertheless, it represents the virtue exactly opposite to the vice of exacerbating the pain inflicted by inequality, that is, to snobbery. The snob eroticizes the social gradient; the gentleman, on the other hand, is solicitous of making the gradient unfelt by those susceptible to feel offended. According to Cardinal John Henry Newman's classical thesis:

> It is almost a definition of a gentleman to say he is one who never inflicts pain. This description is both refined and, as far as it goes, accurate. He is mainly occupied in merely removing the obstacles which hinder the free and unembarrassed action of those about him; and he concurs with their movements rather than takes the initiative himself. His benefits may be considered as parallel to what are called comforts or conveniences in arrangements of a personal nature: like an easy chair or a good fire, which do their part in dispelling cold and fatigue, though nature provides both means of rest and animal heat without them. The true gentleman in like manner carefully avoids whatever may cause a jar or a jolt in the minds of those with whom he is cast; —all clashing of opinion, or collision of feeling, all restraint, or suspicion, or gloom, or resentment; his great concern being to make every one at their ease and at home. (Newman 1852–9, p. 208f)

John Henry Newman is one of the well-known English philosophers who worked on casting the gentleman ideal into an education programme. The list includes names such as Locke, Chesterfield and Shaftesbury. The reason why it was England where philosophers devoted themselves to the gentleman pedagogy was an early demand for intellectual advice. The English aristocracy was put under economic pressure from the uprising bourgeoisie at a far earlier time than their continental cousins. Due to the decline of revenue from large estates, the peerage felt compelled to open the upper

[2]The notion of the Gentleman suffers from ignoble sexism. Gentlemanly qualities, to be sure, have nothing to do with masculinity. A woman can of course be a 'gentleman'. Language, though, denies an adequate genderization. There is no 'gentlelady' in the lexicon. Since attempting to repair the old grammatical injustice of favouring the male form in the designation of universal human qualities by distorting language would just double the embarrassment, we have to make do with the unsightly makeshift of defining the 'gentleman' as timeless and genderless.

ranks of society to social climbers. Admission, of course, was conditional upon the assimilation of polished manners and dignified composure. It was this condition that gave rise to the demand for sophisticated education. The gentleman's distinction lies in his noble character, whose having been fastidiously moulded by an educational programme presupposes a scholarship that understands moral elegance as being at the very core of noblesse. Such an educational programme, accordingly, could not be left to the purview of tutors and educational institutions, but had to be based on philosophical expertise and professional intellectual work. It was in this way that reputed philosophers were given an opportunity to enter, at no risk to their reputation, a saleable genre of advice literature.

Regrettably, though, gentleman pedagogy did not make its way into the textbook philosophy of ethics. The academic discourse remained preoccupied with the opposition of egoism and altruism, the incompatibility between the individual pursuit of interest and the promotion of the common good. The idea of a moral worthy of being obeyed for its own sake was thus overlooked in considerations of the common origin of egocentric and socially-oriented motivations. The idea makes full sense only when developed out of the notion of an inner economy of self-worth, conceived as an embodiment of social context. Without being thus related to the working of self-esteem, personality formation as theorized by gentleman pedagogy risks being dismissed as a luxury problem of high-end social climbers. Without being earthed in the economy of self-worth, the gentleman ideal escapes a thorough investigation of its moral core: the pursuit, quite free of conceitedness, of holding oneself in the highest possible regard.

Relating Elegance to Morality

It is the usefulness of the intrinsic motivation of the morality of the gentleman that means that the admittedly dated ideal merits another look. Though dated, it is not just a high-minded ideal—but one including the aesthetic, if not erotic, appeal to its realization. It unites altruistic and egoistic desirability. Among other reasons, this unification of the supposedly contradictory begs to be reconsidered because it has not even been thoroughly analysed in the original advice literature. The creators of the pertinent pedagogy were prolific in stating rules and providing examples, but they did not go into the architecture of the operating system that integrates the contradictory impulses into a coherent motivation.

Integration means fitting the contradictory impulses together without suppressing or deforming the one or the other. And indeed, my own pursuit of the highest possible opinion of myself is of a striking ambivalence. It can mean to apply for a license to narcissistic self-love as well as to set the standards of one's moral integrity uncompromisingly high. At first glance, this seems to be a blatant contradiction. On closer inspection, however, it turns out that the motivation for the gentleman ideal relies on both parts of the opposition. Its morality does not deny vanity altogether but wisely deals with the powerful drive inherent within it. It translates the contradiction of seductive vice and moral obligation into a complementarity—into properties that are incompatible on the one hand, but on the other hand both necessary for an encompassing description of the phenomenon.[3]

What is still lacking, though, is an explanation of how this complementarity performs. The management of the contradiction of seductive vice and moral obligation makes use of the antagonism of unmediated self-respect and mediated self-esteem, which, in turn, is dynamically integrated into affective self-awareness. The gentleman ideal asks nothing less than turning the antagonism into a relaxed co-operation of self-respect and self-esteem. This translation, to be sure, is a demanding mission. It is demanding with regard to both attractiveness and steadfastness. Mediated self-esteem prescribes building up a winning personality, unmediated self-respect vetoes compromises regarding moral integrity. Pursuing an honest high opinion of oneself asks of us that we excel in both regards. This is about more than just staying upright, decent and morally correct: here, rather, the full range of gentlemanly qualities are required. It means to keep up a level of autonomy that the dependence on other people's value judgement seems to forbid. It means to navigate, without losing poise, the complex dynamics of that network of interdependence that the ego is part of—nay, embodies. In virtue of appearing hopelessly difficult, these requirements disclose why elegance lies at the heart of the gentleman ideal. Elegance is what amazes discreetly: when something difficult is performed with ease, when something laborious is made to look effortless, something complicated quite simple, something artificial as if natural. Elegance masks the unsightly views of our physical and psychic existence, it downplays our clumsiness, fussiness and frailty. Elegance is what a person, a presence, a form of progression is displaying when we are fascinated by a fluency well beyond expectation.[4]

A fluency well beyond expectation covers the 'flow' characteristic of Confucian ease. It encapsulates the noble without dragging its elitist connotations along. Elegance and ease, thus understood, are no upper-class privilege, but the kind of wisdom needed for pursuing one's self-esteem in the complexity of a context that one can neither escape nor control, but that one must not surrender to.[5] This wisdom has nothing particular to do with social climbing or social ambition. It refers to the elites only insofar as it specifies pointedly how they should conduct themselves in a way that shows them worthy of the privileges they enjoy. The wisdom's superiority relies on an unbiased view of the economy of self-worth. By clearly accounting for the dual judgment function of affective self-awareness, it allows the conceptualization of an ethics that dispenses with external motivation.

[3]The paradigm case of complementarity is the wave-particle dualism in quantum theory. Wave and particle are incompatible properties of an entity, but both are necessary for an encompassing description of quantum objects. Complementarity, thus conceived, was introduced by Nils Bohr, who in turn was inspired by a psychological notion thereof that ultimately goes back to William James. On the re-introduction of the concept of complementarity into psychology see Wang and Busemeyer (2015).

[4]cf. Franck 2010

[5]For a scientific account of this basic ambivalence of the human condition see Kauffman (2008).

Elegance, to be sure, is a matter of degree. Moral elegance starts with escaping the bad alternative of either vanity or moral pride in the service of harnessing the psychic energies. Since it would be inelegant, however, to show the effort of control, a more elegant solution would be that the energies are made to control one another. This mutual control is achieved as soon as the repelling opposition relaxes into a countervailing opposition of unmediated self-respect and mediated self-esteem. This relaxation, however, merely marks the bottom line of elegance. To increase the difficulty in order to raise the chances that the performance amazes discreetly, the countervailing opposition must undergo a final sublimation, becoming an outright cooperation for mutual advantage.

The art of behaving in a truly gentlemanly manner lies in utilizing moral standards to perfect the attractiveness of the person, and in employing the psychology of self-esteem to strengthen the immunology of self-respect. The gentleman is aware of the moral significance of the noble. According to Newman's definition, he:

> makes light of favours while he does them, and seems to be receiving when he is conferring. He never speaks of himself except when compelled, never defends himself by a mere retort, he has no ears for slander or gossip, is scrupulous in imputing motives to those who interfere with him, and interprets every thing for the best. He is never mean or little in his disputes, never takes unfair advantage, never mistakes personalities or sharp sayings for arguments, or insinuates evil which he dare not say out. From a long-sighted prudence, he observes the maxim of the ancient sage, that we should ever conduct ourselves towards our enemy as if he were one day to be our friend. (Newman 1852–9, p. 209)

Is it just morally impeccable or rather captivating to earn this description? When saying that the gentleman 'interprets every thing for the best', he adumbrates a principle that is justly called a virtue, but could just as well be called a strategy of raising one's personal charm: *charitable interpretation*. Charitable interpretation means that the interpreter of an utterance, a text, a situation tries hard to find out that one interpretation which makes most sense within the given context. In personal contact, it means trying to find that interpretation of your interlocutor's speech and behaviour that renders them most intelligent, witty and charming: in short, that portrays them in the best possible light. There is little that is as captivating as enjoying charitable interpretation in dealing with an intelligent and sincere partner. And it is certainly not by chance that the philosopher who introduced the principle into the epistemology of understanding, Donald Davidson, gave it this name, with its unmistakable moral overtone (Davidson 1974, Chap. 13; but see also Grice 1975).

Towards an Ethics Tailored to Vanity Fairs

The habit of attempting that interpretation of one's partner's talk and behaviour which renders the person most intelligent, witty and charming is far from being just charitable. It represents, rather, the way in which the upward bias in the valuation of attention can be used to mutual benefit. The more intelligent, witty and charming you allow your partner to prove themself, the higher the value that you have reason to attribute to the attention you receive in the exchange. Your generosity, by improving the position of your partner, thereby ensures you receive your own payment. Both sides find themselves, to a marginal degree at least, upgraded. For society as a whole, this means that the value of the social product of attention exchanged can be increased. It follows, therefore, that the potential for societal welfare is not realized until charitable interpretation becomes the norm rather than the exception. What we thus face is the most natural approach to the ecological problem of the economy of attention. In a society where charitable interpretation defines the default in interpersonal dealings, social capital is safe.

But does this not mean, in reverse, that only societies of gentlemen are well prepared for exploiting the addiction to attention as a major source of motivation? It means, to be sure, that societies that have gone into extensive and systematic exploitation of this addiction expose their members to formidable requirements regarding the management of self-esteem. The gentleman ideal accounts for the ambition of the demands. Its significance lies in the collection of optimality conditions. Societies where lower standards prevail will have trouble with affairs such as the detoxification of the upward bias in the valuation of attention, the demotivation of the false accounting of vanity and resentment, the resistance to the alienating reduction of attention to a currency. A society free of such troubles through affording to utilize vanity fairs might well deserve to be called a society of gentlemen.

Moral elegance, though facilitating the tailoring of an ethics to vanity fairs, is hard to sell as a means of perfecting the attractiveness of the person. Its popularization is hindered by the perfection it imposes: only very few can meet the scrupulous requirements entailed. Yet, the instructions it packages are not so far from simple common sense when considered individually. In a sense, everybody knows that one does best, in the vicissitudes of interpersonal dealings, to keep one's inner household of self-worth relaxed. It is common wisdom that conceit and resentment do not make one happy. Even Confucius' juxtaposition of the noble and the mean only picks up the thread of commonly shared intuitive knowledge. Might it not be, thus, that the route to more practicality is blocked by the tribute the ideal pays to ideal form? Or, asked the other way around, might it be possible to free the ideal from the luxury of its perfection without giving up its basic rationale?

Dispensing with claims of perfection without turning a blind eye to the appeal thereof lies at the base of the socialization of former luxuries. The transmutation of clothing into fashion became possible by way of replacement of custom tailoring with industrial mass manufacture; consumption in the service of prestige ceased to be solely the preserve of upper-class lifestyle through the general transformation of consumer goods into brands. Recently, luxuries deemed essentially tied to privilege—think of working for the wage of fame or glamorous celebrity culture—found themselves socialized, i.e. made accessible to the general public. Would it be frivolous thus to speculate that even the gentleman ideal waits to be socialized by being stripped down to some kind of 'lite' version?

To those dismissing the proposition out of hand, a ready-made rejoinder is in place. The gentleman pedagogy itself started with the socialization of a training which was once a luxury strictly reserved to the courtly world. Yet, this socialization stopped halfway, since it remained restricted to the upper bourgeois section of the social gradient. Hence the tendency of educated politeness to a distinctive mannerism, hence the still elitist stable smell clinging to the image of the gentleman. In other fields, the socialization of former luxury goods and features of upper-class lifestyle went further. Why, accordingly, should the appeal to moral elegance be targeted preferentially to the elites? Why not plead for a completion of the commenced, yet unfinished, socialization?

Elegance intrinsically resists being socialized. Elegance relies on distinction. In contrast to other luxuries, it cannot become ordinary without losing its distinguishing quality. That is why it finds itself replaced in celebrity culture by the less reserved and less discreet alternative: glamour. Glamour, to repeat, is what remains of elegance after subtracting elegant restraint. Glamour is suited for popularization. Elegance is not.

Might this separation be translatable to moral elegance? Are there ways of freeing the ideal from the luxury of perfection without betraying its basic rationale? The polish of manners and elaborate pedagogy are conducive to avoiding the pitfalls with which the management of socially dependent narcissism is riddled—but they do not replace the awareness of the intricate nature of the addiction to attention. The property of moral elegance which waits most eagerly to be socialized is the know-how to make the best of the alleged contradiction between the ego's constitutive claim of autonomy and its no less constitutive dependency on outer esteem.

As such, this know-how is never a question of all or nothing. Its tolerance to being reduced to even quite low levels of aspiration is illustrated by the descent into the ordinary that even a gentleman can afford. You won't risk your standing as a gentleman just by lacking slightly in distinction. To be acknowledged as a gentleman it may be enough to be considered as trustworthy, fair and agreeable in dealing—as being straight as an arrow in all your dealings, with a heart in the right place to boot. The scale of dwindling distinction goes down to what is called 'honour among thieves'. The honour among thieves is the sense of dignity having survived, the baseness of his business notwithstanding, in the criminal's soul.

The sense of dignity is what remains of moral elegance after having left elegant restraint behind. Taken as such, this sense is nothing particular, but present wherever affective self-awareness is awake. The sense of dignity is of the same origin as the very pursuit of attention. In its minimal version, accordingly, it has been popularized since human recollection. It is by refinement along the lines of its own logic, i.e. by elaboration of the economy of self-worth, that it can expand to a secular ethics suited to make inequality bearable, to fight the incentives to false accounting and the alienating reduction of attention.

Self-exploration of the Addiction

The question we thus face is how to strip the know-how elaborated under the banner of moral elegance down to its basic rationale. The core difficulty with which the management of socially dependent narcissism wrestles lies in the unruly nature of the addiction to attention. The approach that suggests itself for getting to the crux of the matter is thus to go a step further into the self-exploration of what the addiction to attention amounts to.

In the case of attention, addiction means much more than insatiability and withdrawal symptoms. It means that the feeling to be the very self one is not only self-referential, but refers also to other, foreign selves. It reveals our instinctive assumption that the ego is not alone in what it feels itself to be—that we cannot help but be concerned with foreign consciousness though forever denied access to it. Temptations to excessiveness and suffering from withdrawal symptoms just underline what our longing for attention reveals about our inborn, natural spirituality. This spirituality is what we testify to inadvertently in our daily dealings with attention. Habitually, to be sure, the testimonial is implicit only. Express awareness to what we testify in deeds is not presupposed. Dealing with fellows as owners of phenomenal consciousness, rather, routinely works in subconscious mode. If our analyses of the economies of self-worth and social standing are correct, even dealings as delicate as the balancing of dependent self-esteem and immediate self-respect are routinely performed without awareness of what they practically presuppose. Routine, nevertheless, borders on carelessness. It forgives discrepancies that do not immediately feel disturbing. By way of routine, the addict degenerates to the junkie; vanity fairs are drug markets indeed. As experienced participants, we tend to be not all too concerned with the social injustice implied in the upward bias, with the self-debasement that opportunistic self-deception incurs, with the erosion of humanity waged by the confusion of attention with another currency. Being all too concerned with subtleties of this nature might even be considered thoroughly unprofessional in business conduct and governance, where assertiveness is expected. Subliminal corruption, thus creeping in, may look affordable if not advisable from the individual's point of view; in sum, however, it often adds up to those collective results whereby more and more individuals no longer recognize the goals they live for.

A secular ethics tailored to vanity fairs should provide guidance on how to deal wisely with the addiction. Since abstaining from the drug is not an option, guidance of how to demotivate those corrupting side-effects is at issue. Carelessness by convenience is an all too human inclination, to be sure, but it is by no means impossible to control. First, awareness or otherwise of the side-effects has no influence on our enjoyment of the drug. Second, there is an antidote that enjoys, perhaps not accidentally, growing popularity in recent times: mindfulness. Mindfulness is the attunement of attention that carefully avoids the thoughtlessness of routine. Even more specifically, mindfulness is key to the practice of every kind of spirituality. With the burgeoning interest in mindfulness has naturally come a growing interest in spirituality. One is no longer suspected of cranky esoterism when confessing to being intrigued by the kind of attentiveness that schools of spirituality have been developing, since time immemorial, for approaching the enigmatic nature of the phenomenal world. Meanwhile, showcased disinterest in spirituality comes across as obtuse. Dedicated students and confessed practitioners of spirituality have already started to complain about an inflation of the use of 'mindfulness' in lifestyle talks. To their dismay, they even observe tendencies of mercantilizing the appeal of spirituality. The key phrase is 'yoga to buy'. Can it be anything but a gross misunderstanding when a notion such as mindfulness becomes a fad? True, mercantile spirituality has little to do with the kind of attentiveness that those schools of spirituality have been developing in order to approach the mystery of mental presence. But what about a more charitable interpretation of the susceptibility to simpler approaches? What if many more people have come to blame the all too common lack of mindfulness for their dissatisfaction with the collective results of the pursuit of attention, than are prepared to undertake a thorough exploration of their addiction? Might these people not be on the way to asking what our culture would be like if dealing wisely with the addiction were a common concern?

The real danger in the offers of easy spirituality lies in their flirting with esoterism. Esoterism is concern with the supernatural. Fascination with the supernatural offers advertising slogans that the wellness industry seems unable to resist. Nothing is more obstructive for self-aware spirituality than contamination with esoterism. The spirituality we have knowledge of by acquaintance has nothing supernatural about it at all. It is as natural as is sentient nature. Sentience is another expression of conscious experience. The minimal form of sentience is the presence of the feeling of what it is like to be the creature one is. Since the feeling of how it is to be might be a constituent of animality as such, sentience might be close to coextensive with animal life. The reason why it is unclear whether sentience is definitely coextensive with animal life is that its existence cannot be proven by empirical method. A creature's sentience is only ever accessible from within, from the perspective of the organism that is itself endowed—or afflicted—with sentience. Within the animal kingdom, nevertheless, there are social animals that have developed a substitute sense for their fellow creatures' sentience: empathy. They have mirror neurons in their brains, enabling them to intuit the 'how it feels' quality of the sentience hidden behind the outer appearance of the conspecific vis-à-vis.

As natural as phenomenal states are as such, just as natural is their social concern. Exploration of what our addiction to attention amounts to thus involves a sharp distinction and a mild revision. Mysteriousness should be sharply distinguished from mysticism. Phenomenal states, though intimately known to us all by acquaintance, are mysterious indeed. Nobody has so far come up with a conclusive, analytically reliable description of what presence, this mode of consciously 'being there', means. Presence, to this day, has stubbornly resisted conclusive definition and thus conceptual analysis (it is not even clear what it would be like to know what presence means in the final analysis). Without conceptual analysis, it is hard to specify the difference that self-aware presence is supposed to make in real life.[6] Even if we have an intuitive idea of the difference that spirituality makes in lifestyle, the challenge of going deeper imposes risks. The risks are either to fail in translating the vague idea into deep insight, or to be simply overwhelmed by the ineffability of what it is like to be mentally present. Definite failure in this translation attempt will likely lead to dismissal of the deeper understanding as a pseudo-problem. The feeling of being simply overwhelmed by the ineffability of what it is like to be mentally present is precisely whence the diehard willingness to see something supernatural in spirituality stems.

The natural way of avoiding both agnosticism and mysticism lies in recognizing natural spirituality as the greatest and most wondrous achievement of biological evolution. The question regarding the difference that self-aware presence is supposed to make in real life should be translated, accordingly, into that of a thought experiment, namely—what would our culture be like if it embraced natural spirituality (instead of dismissing it as nonsense or confounding it with esoterism) as an achievement of natural evolution to be cherished by all with awe for its power, which far eclipses our capacities to grasp it? It is in this question that the ethics we are looking for finds its final test. The model of culture that thus takes shape has an air of utopia, to be sure. But isn't it the straightforward inversion of those dystopian fantasies about leaving behind our sentience-based, naturally-evolved emotionality—if not even biological life—by becoming robots?

Exploration of what the addiction to attention amounts to is a pragmatic way of approaching this lofty question. The addiction, if explored with due care and wisdom, lets us know that we are congenitally equipped to deal with our peers as owners of phenomenal consciousness in a fully aware and appropriate way. Exploring inter-subjectivity with due care and wisdom requires taking notice of the kind of attentiveness that schools of spirituality have been developing for approaching the enigmatic nature of presence as such. The concern with presence other than one's own even suggests a slight revision of the approach. Traditionally, the approach to the nature of presence is practised as meditative immersion into the presence of one's own consciousness. This preoccupation with intra-subjectivity is logical insofar as

---

[6]This is not to say, however, that it is hard to show that deliberate agnosticism has a dehumanizing effect. The effect is demonstrated brutally by a worldview pervasive in our science-minded civilization. The view consists in the seemingly innocent definition of nature as that which natural science describes. The identification of nature with the scope of natural science is known as naturalism. Since sentience has no place in the scope of natural science, this definition of nature amounts to banning sentient nature from nature proper. Deliberative ignorance of sentience may seem arguable on the grounds of the inaccessibility of sentience by empirical method. Basic research and pure theory alike deserve to be shielded against issues they are not equipped to answer. As long as basic research serves exclusively cognitive interests, it arguably can refuse social responsibility for its outcome. Things change when the outcome of knowledge production transcends the province of pure theory. As soon as naturalism turns into a quasi-official worldview of technologically advanced societies, denial of sentient nature means to give the blessing to ruthless brutality toward animals on industrial scale. How dehumanizing deliberate ignorance can be is demonstrated by the cruelty to animals inherent in intensive farming and the unscrupulous processing of sensitive tissue in the meat and fish industries. Dismissing natural spirituality is much more than just shortsightedness. It is a serious threat to the nature we are part of ourselves. Loosening the blindfold is an ethical command far exceeding the domain of vanity fairs.

phenomenal states are accessible only from within. It did not prevent acknowledgement of the communality of phenomenal states in the form of, e.g. commandments of respect or even unconditional love of sentient creatures. Nevertheless, acknowledgement of the social dimension of the very feeling to be the creature one is has remained overshadowed by deepened inwardness. Witness the endeavours, characteristic of cultures of spirituality worldwide, to abjure the pursuit of attention.

To bring the latent spirituality of our daily dealings with attention to light, these reservations must be turned, without diminishing the attentiveness to the spiritual as such, into a positive, marvelling openness. What appeals to be heard is nothing less than the basic, libidinal tone of one's own consciousness. A tone which is by nature susceptible to the affection of others. Sure, attentiveness to this basic, libidinal tone risks being confused with a detraction from the mystery of mental presence as such. On closer inspection, however, the mystery doubles. Self-awareness of mental presence includes an awareness that this presence, though windowless, is not self-contained. Witness the withdrawal symptoms hijacking the soul when it feels abandoned by other souls of its ilk. By inferring back from the addiction to the drug, we see what it is that makes us downright 'high' when feeling that the drug works. Aren't we facing the kind of reaction of own and other as epitomized by the shiver of romantic eye contact? And doesn't attentiveness to the eroticism emanating from one's own imagination of being welcomed in another consciousness come very close to a meditation on foreign-owned presence?

Conclusion

A culture in possession of the means to thoroughly commercialize the economy of attention, yet feeling encouraged to fade out the spiritual dimension of peoples' concern for their role in fellow consciousness suffers from a consequential mismatch. It is at a loss as to how to make use of what it factually presupposes. It employs socially dependent narcissism as a functional kind of greed. What fall victim to this reduction are the most culturally significant intricacies of the social dependency of humans' feeling of self. It is by caring about one's role in fellow consciousness in a much deeper way than mere formal dressage that agreeably cultivated manners are acquired. How beneficial and genial life in society can be depends on how common the understanding is that we have to do with one another as embodied souls.

Something quite basic must have gone awry when a culture preoccupied with the handling of attention is blamed for a widely felt lack of mindfulness. Dealing with attention mindfully starts with becoming aware of that on which its potential as a drug relies. Where such understanding does not impose restraint, the drug's quality of attention invites relentless exploitation for reasons of profit. Socially dependent narcissism indeed proves a fertile source of profit where attention is reduced to currency and measure of social status, where the pursuit of attention is run as a capitalist economy, where Matthew effectiveness and resentment flourish as proven strategies of enrichment. These strategies not only give expression to a proliferating business mentality, they are also expressive of a pervasive coarsening and savaging of common manners—a decline sensibly attributed to a lack of mindfulness.

It is hopeless, of course, to do away with mental capitalism. This does not mean, however, that it is pointless to inquire as to the difference that ethics makes in dealing with attention. The question rather is with what kind of ethics must we gird ourselves to fight the dehumanizing effects of economic rationalization. Is there an ethics suited to turn socially dependent narcissism from a fertile source of profit into an agent of the common good? The answer we have been approaching is quite clear. Yes, it is an ethics the first commandment of which is that those participating in the economy of attention ought to live in full awareness of the spirituality they naturally share. Concern about our place in the consciousness of others is inborn: awareness of the spiritual dimension of this concern provides the consummate means of detoxifying the upward bias in the valuation of attention, of demotivating the false accounting of vanity and resentment, and of overcoming the alienating reduction of attention.

References

Aristotle. 2011. *The Eudemian Ethics*, trans. Anthony Kenny, Oxford: Oxford World's Classics.

Confucius. 2009. *The Confucian Analects, the Great Learning & the Doctrine of the Mean*, trans. James Legge, New York: Cosimo.

Davidson, Donald. 1974. *On the Very Idea of a Conceptual Scheme: Inquiries into Truth and Interpretation*. Oxford: Clarendon Press.

Graaff, J. de V. 1957. *Theoretical Welfare Economics*. London: Cambridge University Press.

Grice, Paul H. 1975. Logic and Conversation. In *Syntax and Semantics*, vol. 3, *Speech Acts*, ed. Peter Cole, and Jerry L. Morgan, 41–58. New York: Academic Press.

Kauffman, Stuart. 2008. *Reinventing the Sacred: A New View of Science, Reason, and Religion*. New York: Basic Books.

Newman, John Henry. 1852–9. *The Idea of a University*. London. Reprint Dublin: Ashfield, 2009.

Peil Kauffman, Katherine T. 2012. *Emotion: A Self-Regulatory Sense?* FTS International. Available at www.emotionalsentience.com).

Wang, Zheng, and Jerome Busemeyer. 2015. Reintroducing the Concept of Complementarity Into Psychology. In *Frontiers in Psychology*, vol. 6 (Nov 2015), article 1822 (www.frontiersin.org).

Bibliography

Adorno, Theodor W. 1958/1991. Short Commentaries on Proust. In *idem, Notes to Literature*, vol. 1. Trans. by Shierry Weber Nicholson, 174–184. New York: Columbia University Press (originally published as: Kleine Proust-Kommentare, in: Akzente, 1958, no. 6, pp. 564ff).

Anissimov, Michael. 2007. *Objections to Coherent Extrapolated Volition*. Singularity Institute for Artificial Intelligence.

Aristotle. 2011. *The Eudemian Ethics*, trans. Anthony Kenny, Oxford: Oxford World's Classics.

Bataille, Georges. 1967. *The Accursed Share*, vol. 1, translated from French by Robert Hurley, New York: Zone Books.

Becker, Gary S. 1976. *The Economic Approach to Human Behaviour*. Chicago and London: Chicago University Press.

Bonitz, M., E. Bruckner, and A. Scharnhorst. 1997. Characteristics and Impact of the Matthew Effect for Countries. *Scientometrics* 40 (3): 407–422.

Bostrom, Nick. 2014. *Superintelligence: Paths, Dangers, Strategies*. Oxford: Oxford University Press.

Bourdieu, Pierre. 1979/1984. *Distinction: A Social Critique of the Judgement of Taste*. Trans. Richard Nice. Cambridge, MA: Harvard University Press.

Bourdieu, Pierre. 1986. The Forms of Capital. In *Handbook of Theory and Research for the Sociology of Education*, ed. John G. Richardson, 241–258. New York: Greenwood Press.

Brin, Sergey, and Lawrence Page. 1998. *The Anatomy of a Large-Scale Hypertextual Web Search Engine*. http://infolab.stanford.edu/backrub/google.html.

Buchanan, James M., and Gordon Tullock. 1962. *The Calculus of Consent: Logical Foundation of Constitutional Democracy*. Ann Arbor: University of Michigan Press.

Chalmers, David J. 1995. Facing up to the Problem of Consciousness. *Journal of Consciousness Studies* 2 (3): 200–219.

Chalmers, David J. 2000. What is a Neural Correlate of Consciousness? In *Neural Correlates of Consciousness*, ed. Thomas Metzinger, 17–39. Cambridge: MIT Press.

Citton, Yves. 2017. *The Ecology of Attention*. Trans. From French by Barnaby Norman. Cambridge, UK, Malden, MA: Polity Press.

Confucius. 2009. *The Confucian Analects, the Great Learning & the Doctrine of the Mean*, trans. James Legge, New York: Cosimo.

de Solla Price, Derek J. 1963. *Little Science, Big Science*. New York: Columbia University Press.

de Saussure, Ferdinand. 1916. *Course in general linguistics*. Translated from French by Roy Harris, La Salle, Ill.: Open Court, 1983.

de Vany, Arthur. 2004. *Hollywood Economics. How Extreme Uncertainty Shapes the Film Industry.* London and New York: Routledge.

Davenport, Thomas H., and John C. Beck. 2001. *The Attention Economy. Understanding the New Currency of Business*. Boston: Harvard Business School Press.

G. Franck, *Vanity Fairs*,
https://doi.org/10.1007/978-3-030-41532-7

Davidson, Donald. 1974. *On the Very Idea of a Conceptual Scheme: Inquiries into Truth and Interpretation*. Oxford: Clarendon Press.

Dennett, Daniel C. 1994, September 1–3. Consciousness in Human and Robot Minds. In *IIAS Symposium on Cognition, Computation and Consciousness, Kyoto*; online http://ase.tufts.edu/cogstud/dennett/papers/concrobt.htm.

Derrida, Jacques. 1967/1997. *Of Grammatology, Original in French: De la Grammatologie*. Paris: Les Éditions de Minuit, 1967; Translated into English by Gayatri Chakravorty Spivak. Baltimore, London: Johns Hopkins University Press, 1997 (corrected edition).

Descartes, Renée. 1637, 1968. *Discourse on Method and the Meditations*. Trans. E.F. Sutcliffe. London et al.: Penguin.

Downs, Anthony. 1957. *An Economic Theory of Democracy*. New York, NY: Harper & Row.

Eisenman, Peter. 1995. *Aura und Exzess: Zur Überwindung der Metaphysik der Architektur. Essays und Gespräche 1976–1994*. Vienna: Passagen Architektur.

Falkinger, Josef. 2005, March. Limited Attention as the Scarce Resource in an Information-Rich Society, IZA Discussion Paper No. 1538.

Fengler, Susanne, and Stephan Ruß-Mohl. 2008. Journalists and the Information-Attention Markets: Towards an Economic Theory of Journalism. *Journalism*, 2008—http://journals.sagepub.com.

Franck, Dorothea. 2016. A Plea for Awareness: Mind Your Emotional Footprint. https://dorotheafranck.wordpress.com/a-plea-for-awareness-watch-your-emotional-footprint-2/.

Franck, Dorothea, and Georg Franck. 1986. Zwischenmenschliche Verhandlung versus intersubjektive Norm. Für eine Analytik des Sprecherwechsels als nicht regelgeleiteter Selbstorganisation des Gesprächs. *Papiere zur Linguistik 35* (Heft 2/1986).

Franck, Dorothea, and Georg Franck. 2001. *Quality: On the Poetics of Architecture*. English Trans. Qualität. Von der poetischen Kraft der Architektur. Appeared in Merkur, no. 626, June 2001. Translation available under http://www.iemar.tuwien.ac.at/publications.

Franck, Georg. 1989, August. Die neue Währung: Aufmerksamkeit. Zum Einfluss der Hochtechnik auf Zeit und Geld (The new Currency: Attention. On the Influence of High Technology on Time and Money). *Merkur 486*: 688–701.

Franck, Georg. 1993, September/October/2018. The economy of attention (English translation of "Ökonomie der Aufmerksamkeit". *Merkur 534/535*: 748–761, translated by Silvia Plaza and Robert van Krieken, *Journal of Sociology 55* (1), 2018, pp. 8–19.

Franck, Georg. 1998. *Die Ökonomie der Aufmerksamkeit* (The Economy of Attention). Munich: Carl Hanser Verlag

Franck, Georg. 1999. Scientific Communication: A Vanity Fair? *Science* 286 (5437): 53–55.

Franck, Georg. 2002. The Scientific Economy of Attention: A Novel Approach to the Collective Rationality of Science. *Scientometrics* 55 (1): 3–26.

Franck, Georg. 2003. How time passes. On conceiving time as a process. In: *The Nature of Time: Geometry, Physics and Perception (NATO Science Series II)* ed. R. Buccheri, M. Saniga and W.M. Stuckey, vol. 95, 91–103. Dordrecht: Kluwer Academic.

Franck, Georg. 2005a. *Mentaler Kapitalismus (Mental Capitalism)*. Munich: Carl Hanser.

Franck, Georg. 2005b. Mental Capitalism. In: *What People Want. Populism in Architecture and Design*, ed. Michael Shamiyeh and DOM Research Laboratory; Basel, Boston & Berlin: Birkhäuser, 98–115. Reprinted in D.A. A Transdisciplinary Handbook of Design Anthropology, ed. Yana Milev, 580-596. Frankfurt/Main: Peter Lang, 2013.

Franck, Georg. 2008. Presence and reality. An option to specify panpsychism? *Mind and Matter* 6: 123–140.

Franck, Georg. 2010. Eleganz. Ein Abgesang (Elegance. A swan's song). In: *Merkur no. 739* (December 2010), pp. 1208–1211.

Franck, Georg. 2011. Celebrity and Populism. In: *Elmgreen & Dragset, Trilogy*, ed. Peter Weibel and Andreas F. Beitin, 112–122. Köln: Walter König, and Karlsruhe: ZKM | Center for Art and Media Karlsruhe.

Franck, Georg. 2012. What Kind of Being is Mental Presence? Toward a Novel Analysis of the Hard Problem of Consciousness. *Mind and Matter* 10 (1): 7–24.

Franck, Georg. 2015. The Wage of Fame: How Non-Epistemic Motives Have Enabled the Phenomenal Success of Modern Science. *Gerontology* 61(1):89–94.
Franck, Georg. 2016a. Vigilance: Embodied Nowness? On the Relation of Mental Presence to Time and Energy. *Intellectica 66*: 125–138.
Franck, Georg. 2016b. Vanity Fairs. Competition in the Service of Self-Esteem. *Mind and Matter 14* (2): 155–165.
Franck, Georg. 2017. Resonanz und Ressentiment (resonance and resentment), in: NZZ dated 6.2.2017, no. 30, p. 8 (International edition dated 7.2.2017, p. 17)
Franck, Georg, and Harald Atmanspacher. 2009. A Proposed Relation Between Intensity of Presence and Duration of Nowness. In: *Recasting Reality. Wolfgang Pauli's Philosophical Ideas and Contemporary Science*, ed. Harald Atmanspacher & Hans Primas, 211–225. Berlin & Heidelberg: Springer.
Goldhaber, Michael. 1997. The economy of attention and the Net. *First Monday, 2* (4), 7 Apr 1997.
Graaff, J. de V. 1957. *Theoretical Welfare Economics*. London: Cambridge University Press.
Grice, Paul H. 1975. Logic and Conversation. In *Syntax and Semantics*, vol. 3, *Speech Acts*, ed. Peter Cole, and Jerry L. Morgan, 41–58. New York: Academic Press.
Hagstrom, Warren O. 1966. *The Scientific Community*. New York: Basic Books.
Hardin, Garrett. 1968. The Tragedy of the Commons. *Science* 162: 1243–1248.
Huberman, Bernardo A., Daniel M. Romero, and Wu Fang. 2009. Crowdsourcing, Attention and Productivity. *Journal of Information* 35 (6): 758–765.
Hughes, J. 2010. *Problems of Transhumanism: Liberal Democracy vs. Technocratic Absolutism*. Institute for Ethics and Emerging Technologies. https://ieet.org/index.php/IEET2/print/3670.
Husserl, Edmund. 1935. *The Crisis of European Sciences and Transcendental Phenomenology: An Introduction to Phenomenological Philosophy*. Trans. David Carr. Evanston, Ill.: Northwestern University Press, 1970.
James, William. 1890. *The Principles of Psychology*. New York: Henry Holt.
Jordan, J.S., and M. Ghin. 2006. (Proto-) consciousness as a Contextually-Emergent Property of Self-sustaining Systems. *Mind & Matter* 4 (1): 45–68.
Jordan, J.S., and D. Vinson. 2012. After Nature: On Bodies, Consciousness, and Causality. *Journal of Consciousness Studies* 19: 229–250.
Jordan, Scott, and Georg Franck. 2017. Wild Presence. *Mind and Matter* 15 (1): 131–141.
Kant, Immanuel. 1784. Idea for a Universal History with a Cosmopolitan Purpose. In Reiss, H. S., Kant. *Cambridge Texts in the History of Political Thought*, 41–53, 2nd ed, eds. H.S. Reiss, and Kant. Cambridge: Cambridge University Press.
Kauffman, Stuart. 2008. *Reinventing the Sacred: A New View of Science, Reason, and Religion*. New York: Basic Books.
Kitcher, Philip. 1993. *The Advancement of Science: Science without Legend, Objectivity without Illusions*. New York: Oxford UP.
Kurzweil, Ray. 2005. *The Singularity is Near: When Humans Transcend Biology*. New York et al.: Penguin.
Lasch, Christopher 1979. *The Culture of Narcissism*. London: Abacus.
Leary, Mark R., Ellen S. Tambor, Sonja K. Terdal, and Deborah L. Downs. 1995. Self-esteem as an Interpersonal Monitor: The Sociometer Hypothesis. *Journal of Personality and Social Psychology* 68 (3): 518–530.
Lewis, David. 1969. *Convention: A Philosophical Study*. Cambridge, MA: Harvard University Press.
Loos, Adolf. 2009. *Warum die Architektur keine Kunst ist*. Reprint Vienna: Metroverlag.
Lotka, Alfred J. 1926. The Frequency Distribution of Scientific Productivity. *Journal of the Washington Academy of Sciences* 16 (12): 317.
Mach, Ernst. 1883. *The Science of Mechanics*. Chicago: The Open Court Publishing Co., 1911.
Maslow, A. 1943. A Theory of Human Motivation. *Psychological Review* 50: 370–396.
Mauss, Marcel. 1925. *The Gift*, translated from French by Jane I. Guyer, Chicago: Hau Books.
Mead, George Herbert. 1934. *Mind, self, and society*. Chicago & London: Chicago University Press.
Merton, Robert K. 1968. The Matthew Effect in Science. *Science* 159: 56–62.

Merton, Robert K. 1973. *The Sociology of Science*. Chicago: Chicago UP.
Nagel, Thomas. 1974. What is it Like to be a Bat? *Philosophical Review* 83: 181–195.
Newman, John Henry. 1852–9. *The Idea of a University*. London. Reprint Dublin: Ashfield, 2009.
Niskanen, William A. 1968. Nonmarket Decision Making: The Peculiar Economics of Bureaucracy. *The American Economic Review* 58 (2): 293–305.
Ostrom, Elinor. 1990. *Governing the Commons: The Evolution of Institutions of Collective Action*. Cambridge: Cambridge University Press.
Pashler, Harold. 1998. *The Psychology of Attention*. Cambridge, MA: MIT Press.
Pasquinelli, Matteo. 2009. Google's PageRank Algorithm: A Diagram of the Cognitive Capitalism and the Rentier of the Common Intellect. In Deep Search: The Politics of Search Beyond Google, eds. Konrad Becker, and Felix Stalder. London: Transaction Publishers, 2009.
Peil Kauffman, Katherine T. 2012. *Emotion: A Self-Regulatory Sense?* FTS International. Available at www.emotionalsentience.com).
Popper, Karl. 1934/1959. *The Logic of Scientific Discovery*. London, New York: Routledge. Original published in German in 1934; first English translation in 1959.
Primas, Hans. 2009. Complementarity of mind and matter. In *Recasting Reality. Wolfgang Pauli's Philosophical Ideas and Contemporary Science* ed. Harald Atmanspacher & Hans Primas, 171–209. Springer: Berlin & Heidelberg.
Putnam, Robert D. 1995. Bowling Alone: America's Declining Social Capital. *Journal of Democracy* 6: 64–78.
Pylkkänen, Paavo. 2014. Can Quantum Analogies Help us to Understand the Process of Thought? *Mind and Matter* 12 (1): 61–91.
Ravetz, Jerome R. 1971. *Scientific Knowledge and Its Social Problems*. Oxford: Clarendon Press (new edition: London: Transaction Publishers 1996).
Rescher, Nicholas. 1989. *Cognitive Economy: The Economic Dimension of the Theory of Knowledge*. Pittsburgh: Pittsburgh University Press.
Rizzolatti, Giacomo., and Laila, Craighero. 2004. The mirror-neuron system. *Annual Review of Neuroscience* 27 (1): 169–192.
Ryle, Gilbert. 2002. *The Concept of Mind (1949)*. Chicago: The University of Chicago Press (new edition: Chicago UP).
Samuelson, Paul A. 1947. *Foundations of Economic Analysis*. Cambridge, Massachusetts: Harvard University Press.
Samuelson, Paul A. 1954, November. The Pure Theory of Public Expenditure. The Review of Economics and Statistics 36(4): 387–389.
Simon, Herbert A. 1971. Designing Organisations for an Information-Rich World. In *Computers, Communications and the Public Interest*, ed. M. Greenberger, 38–52. Baltimore: Johns Hopkins Press.
Spiekermann, Sarah, Mark Coeckelbergh, Charles M. Ess, Georg Franck, Peter Hampson, and Johannes Hoff. 2017. The Ghost of Transhumanism & the Sentience of Existence. In *Research-Gate Technical Report*. https://www.researchgate.net/publication/318377886_The_Ghost_of_Transhumanism_the_Sentience_of_Existence.
Stockman, David. 2013. The Great Deformation, Public Affairs Symposium on 'Conversation with Zombies'. *Journal of Consciousness Studies* 2 (4): 312–372.
Van Krieken, Robert. 2019. *Celebrity Society*. The Struggle for Attention. 2nd ed., New York: Routledge.
Veblen, Thorstein. 1899. *The Theory of the Leisure Class: An Economic Study of Institutions. Introduction by Stuart Chase*. New York: The Modern Library, 1934.
Vellay, Marc, and Kenneth Frampton. 1985. *Pierre Chareau. Architect and Craftsman 1883–1950*. London: Thames & Hudson.
Walker, Stephen. 1983. *Animal Thought*. London: Routledge.
Wang, Zheng, and Jerome Busemeyer. 2015. Reintroducing the Concept of Complementarity Into Psychology. In *Frontiers in Psychology*, vol. 6 (Nov 2015), article 1822 (www.frontiersin.org).

Wu, Tim. 2016. *The Attention Merchants. The Epic Scramble to Get Inside our Heads*. New York: Alfred A. Knopf.

Yudkowsky, Eliezer. 2008. Artificial Intelligence as a Positive and Negative Factor in Global Risk. In *Global Catastrophic Risks*, ed. Nick Bostrom, and Milan M. Ćirković, 308–345. New York: Oxford University Press.

Index

G. Franck, *Vanity Fairs*,
https://doi.org/10.1007/978-3-030-41532-7

F

G

T

The manufacturer's authorised representative in the EU is Springer Nature Customer Service Centre GmbH, Europaplatz 3, 69115 Heidelberg, Germany. If you have any concerns regarding our products, please contact ProductSafety@springernature.com

Printed and bound by CPI Group (UK) Ltd, Croydon, CR0 4YY
30/09/2026
02225608-0010